ᴨh

Notting Hill Editions is an independent British publisher. The company was founded by Tom Kremer (1930–2017), champion of innovation and the man responsible for popularising the Rubik's Cube.

After a successful business career in toy invention Tom decided, at the age of eighty, to fulfil his passion for literature. In a fast-moving digital world Tom's aim was to revive the art of the essay, and to create exceptionally beautiful books that would be lingered over and cherished.

Hailed as 'the shape of things to come', the family-run press brings to print the most surprising thinkers of past and present. In an era of information-overload, these collectible pocket-size books distil ideas that linger in the mind.

Margaret Atwood, whose work has been published in more than forty-five countries, is the author of more than fifty books of fiction, poetry, critical essays and graphic novels. *Dearly*, her first collection of poetry in over a decade, was published in November 2020. Her latest novel, *The Testaments*, was a co-winner of the 2019 Booker Prize. Her other works of fiction include *Cat's Eye*, finalist for the 1989 Booker Prize; *Alias Grace*, which won the Giller Prize in Canada and the Premio Mondello in Italy; *The Blind Assassin*, winner of the 2000 Booker Prize; *The MaddAddam Trilogy*; and *Hag-Seed*. She is the recipient of numerous awards, including the Peace Prize of the German Book Trade, the Franz Kafka International Literary Prize, the PEN Center USA Lifetime Achievement Award and the *Los Angeles Times* Innovator's Award. She lives in Toronto.

Elliot Ross has been a photographic artist for over fifty years. He is the author of the critically acclaimed monographs *Animal* and *Other Animals* and his work is in the collections of The Center for Creative Photography, Tucson; The Bibliothèque Nationale, Paris; The Musée de la Photographie, Charleroi, Belgium; The Museum of Fine Arts, Houston; and other museums. He lives in San Francisco and New York with his wife, writer Ellen Ullman. He began photographing animals in 2006 when, after the family cat Sadie died, Ullman put up a snapshot of her, which led Ross to wonder about what Sadie had been thinking as she looked into the lens, and later on, about what we can ever know about another species' thoughts and emotions. (www.elliotross.com)

ON CATS
An Anthology

–

Introduced by
Margaret Atwood

Photographs by
Elliot Ross

Edited by
Suzy Robinson

 Notting Hill Editions

Published in 2021
by Notting Hill Editions Ltd
Mirefoot, Burneside, Kendal LA8 9AB

Series design by FLOK Design, Berlin, Germany
Cover design by Plain Creative, Kendal
Creative Advisor: Dennis PAPHITIS

Typeset by CB Editions, London
Printed and bound by Memminger MedienCentrum, Memmingen,
Germany

A CIP record for this book is available from the British Library

ISBN 978-1-912559-32-9

www.nottinghilleditions.com

Cats are intended to teach us that not everything in nature has a purpose.

– Garrison Keillor

Contents

– Introduction –

xi

– TOVE JANSSON –

from The Summer Book

1

– HILAIRE BELLOC –

from A Conversation with a Cat, and Others

9

– ANONYMOUS –

Pangur Bán (The Monk and his Cat)

15

– LOU ANDREAS-SALOMÉ –

from The Freud Journal of Lou Andreas-Salomé

16

– ERNEST HEMINGWAY –

Letter to Hadley Mowrer, 25 November 1943

18

– LYNNE TRUSS –

from Making the Cat Laugh: One Woman's
Journal of Single Life on the Margins

22

– LEWIS CARROLL –

from Alice's Adventures in Wonderland

27

– DORIS LESSING –

from Particularly Cats

31

– RING LARDNER –

It Looks Bad for the Three Little Lardner Kittens

41

– NAOMI FRY –

Mog the Cat and the Mysteries of Animal
Subjectivity

47

– MURIEL SPARK –

from Robinson

54

– EDWARD GOREY –

from The Cat on My Shoulder:
Writers and their Cats

58

– CAITLIN MORAN –

A Death in the Family

62

– OLIVER SODEN –
from Jeoffry: The Poet's Cat
66

– CHRISTINA ROSSETTI –
On the Death of a Cat, a Friend of Mine,
Aged Ten Years and a Half
75

– MARY GAITSKILL –
from Lost Cat
77

– URSULA K. LE GUIN –
from My Life So Far, By Pard
88

– REBECCA WEST –
from Why My Mother was Frightened of Cats
95

– THE REVEREND HENRY ROSS –
An Inscription at St. Augustine with
St. Faith's Church
107

– BOHUMIL HRABAL –
from All My Cats
109

– GUY DE MAUPASSANT –
from On Cats
117

– JOHN KEATS –
To Mrs. Reynolds' Cat
121

– JAMES BOWEN –
from A Street Cat Named Bob
122

– NIKOLA TESLA –
from A Story of Youth Told by Age
127

– BROTHERS GRIMM –
Cat and Mouse in Partnership
132

– ALICE WALKER –
from Frida, The Perfect Familiar
137

Cat-echisms
144

MARGARET ATWOOD

– Introduction –

I was a cat-deprived young child. I longed for a
kitten, but was denied one: we spent two thirds
of every year in the north woods of Canada, so if we
took the cat with us it would run away and get lost
and be eaten by wolves; but if we did not take it with
us, who would look after it?

These objections were unanswerable. I bided my
time. Meanwhile I fantasised. My drawings as a six-
year-old are festooned with flying cats, and my first
book – a volume of poems put together with folded
sheets and a construction-paper cover – was called
Rhyming Cats, and had an illustration of a cat playing with a ball. This cat looked like a sausage with
ears and whiskers, but it was early days in my design
career.

Then our months spent in the woods became
fewer, and I saw an opening. A cat belonging to one
of my friends had kittens. Could I, would they, can't
I, why not? I wore them down. My father was never
entirely easy about having an indoor cat – he was
born at the beginning of the twentieth century on
a small backwoods farm, so for him cats belonged
in the barn, their job was to catch rats and mice,
and unwanted kittens were drowned in a sack – but

he conceded that this particular cat was unusually agreeable and intelligent, for a cat.

This cat's name was Percolator. (A pun of sorts. I expect you noticed.) Her nickname was Perky, and she lived up to it, being alert and energetic. She slept in the dolls' bed in my room – never much used for dolls – or else on top of me, and I loved her dearly. In those days we didn't yet know that we should not let cats outside due to their devastating effect on wild bird populations, so Perky went in and out at night through my ground-floor bedroom window, and brought me nocturnal presents. The presents were things she had caught. If mice, they were usually dead, but several birds were not, and had to be pursued around the room, captured, and rescued via shoebox hospital. If the interventions were successful the birds would be released in the morning; if not, there would be burials. Once there was a rabbit, which did not have any bite marks on it as such, and gave me and also Perky a lively chase before being inserted into the shoebox. Unfortunately, it died anyway, probably of shock. (Grabbed by a monster. Incarcerated by an alien. You can see how upsetting that would have been.)

In the summers, when we went to the north woods, our next-door neighbour, Rhea, kindly fed Perky, who seemed to be able to fend quite well for herself outside. There was an abandoned orchard nearby and a cemetery within reach, so she had ample hunting grounds. All went well until the day of Rhea's garden party. The women in their flowered dresses and sunhats were seated around a large low table, on which there was a platter of stuffed dates rolled in powdered sugar. Oblong, moist. Perky, to show gratitude, brought a gift – a dead mole, well-licked and smoothed, also oblong and moist – and laid it on the platter. Someone almost ate it. You can imagine. (But still, how clever!)

Then, when I was almost twelve, I had a baby sister. This event spelled doom for Perky. One day when I came home from school she was not there. She'd been caught licking milk from the baby's mouth, and, fearful that she would sit on the baby's head and smother her, my parents had 'given her away'. I expect this had meant a trip to the Humane Society and a swift death, but I never knew. Nowadays there would be a family consultation and much empathetic explaining, no doubt, though the cat would have been done away with anyway. As it was, this was a tragedy, a thunderbolt from Zeus; and like a thunderbolt from Zeus, there was no sense in questioning it. Did I resent this disappearance of my first cat? I did. Have I ever forgotten it? As you can see, I haven't. How could I have been so heartlessly severed from my animal daemon in this way? But so it was.

Other cats followed, though much later: hard to have a cat when you are living in residences, rooming houses, and rented apartments that said NO PETS.

But after a while along came Patience, who got stuck all over with burrs and then rolled on the afghan I had just painstakingly knitted; and Ruby, the tough, formidable senior we inherited when we moved to a farm, and who used to go for walks with us like a dog.

Then, suddenly, I had a small child of my own, and she too was afflicted with longing for a cat. The inevitable was staved off for a short period: there was already a mouse in the household. It cannot be said to have been very friendly: it went round and round on its exercise wheel, bit fingers, and from time to time emitted foul smells. But then the mouse died. It was being shown off to two visiting boys, and a skit from Monty Python ensued.

'This mouse is dead!'

'No it isn't, it's sleeping.'

'Look! Dead!' (Pokes mouse.)

Was there trauma? There was not. The mouse was given a formal burial in the back yard, complete with songs, and was known to have gone to heaven because squeaking was heard high above. (Chimney swifts, I expect.) The grave was then re-opened, and behold, no mouse was in it! (Dirt from the covering sod had concealed it.) Two minutes later: 'Now that the mouse is dead, can I have a kitten?'

A neighbour had some, and was more than happy to part with two, 'So they will have someone to play with.' Naming rights were given to the five-year-old. One kitten was grey and fluffy, and was named Fluffy. The other was short-haired and black, and was named Blackie. Not sophisticated names, to be sure – no Oedipus, no Octopus, no Platypus, no Catatonic – but descriptive. These kittens were remarkably patient, and allowed themselves to be stuffed into dolls' dresses and wheeled around in a toy buggy. (I had done the same to Perky, so who was I to tut-tut?) The rule was that they should not be allowed outside in these costumes, as they might get caught on branches and strangle on their bonnet strings, but occasionally they would escape, and passersby would be treated to the sight of one of them in a pinafore and flouncy hat, leaping from rooftop to rooftop at the second-storey level.

Fluffy was obliging, Blackie was a con artist. He used to sneak over to one of the neighbours and mew piteously, pretending to be lost. They would let him in and feed him. It took them a while to figure out that he lived a mere two doors down. When, shortly after that, we moved to a different address, it did not take him long to try out the new neighbours, but with an added touch: he would stick his paw inside his collar and demand to be rescued. Fluffy, meanwhile, was working the sidewalk beat, lolling around voluptuously, inviting pedestrians to rub her belly, and attracting treats. Ring of doorbell: total stranger. 'Please tell Fluffy I'm so sorry I forgot her smoked salmon today, but I'll bring it tomorrow.'

Children grow up and go away, and parents inherit the cats. This happens faster than you'd think. In no time at all I had two familiars. Fluffy claimed the stairway, and would contest this space with Blackie when he was going up or down; but Blackie owned my study, and would help me write, as cats do, by climbing onto the keyboard, messing up loose papers, or twanging the elastic bands around manuscripts. Neither of them were hunters. Squirrels would bounce off Blackie as he lay dozing, enticing him to chase them, but he would merely blink. Mice would appear in the kitchen – they'd come up a drainpipe, before we got that fixed – and Blackie and Fluffy would just stare at them. ('Blackie! Fluffy! Do your thing!' Looks of disdain: what were they, peasants?)

Though they were not devoid of defensive skills. I once saw the two of them watch an approaching and evil-intentioned raccoon – stalk still, tails twitching slightly – until the very last minute, when they flew at the intruder's nose, all claws unsheathed. It was like something out of a John Keegan warfare strategy book: Keep together! Hold the line! Don't fire until you see the whites of their eyes! No retreat! Attaaack!

There must have been confrontations with other cats, as well. In nature the territory for a male cat is a square mile. No wonder there are cat fights in cities. Blackie probably lost most of his fights: he was a wily Ulysses, not a brawny Achilles. Once he came home with a claw stuck into his nose. ('Blackie! What have you been up to?' Heart-rending mew.) Torn ears and missing patches of fur and skin had to be doctored.

Writers and their cats – it's a theme. There have been books of photos dedicated to it. There are also writers and their dogs, writers and their birds – parrots and ravens feature – and perhaps (I'm guessing) writers and their snakes, but I'd bet that the cats predominate. They interview well, projecting a mysterious aura while giving away exactly nothing. They hold still for the camera; they do not splash around in mud puddles and then jump all over the journalist; they do not pant and drool. Like all proper Romantics they are independent-minded, and Byronic in their contempt for authority. They are always well-groomed.

Are they Influences? Are they Muses? Yes and no, depending how you count. They certainly get into stories and poems, or at least they have gotten into mine. Not always 'my' cats, however: sometimes the cats of others. One cat – true story – belonged to a friend of mine; it was kidnapped by a vengeful ex and imprisoned in a locking-lid metal garbage can. (Happy-ending rescue after a frantic search and some 'help me' meowing.) A wish-fulfilment piece of mine called 'Our Cat Enters Heaven' features Blackie in disguise, and informs us that God is a large cat. Or such would be the form in which he or she would surely appear to a cat.

This story was one of many iterations of my period of mourning after Blackie died. That is the downside to having a cat: cats die, most usually before you yourself do. I'm not sure why I was so flattened after the death of this particular cat, but I was.

The event occurred while we were away. My sister had been doing cat care, and Blackie had developed a kidney disease. Yes, it could be treated, said the vet, but Blackie would have to be given a needle twice a day and have a urine sample collected. What were the odds on that? Zero. One needle and Blackie would not have waited around for the second. He'd have been off to the shrubbery at first chance. As for the urine sample: 'Blackie, pee in the bottle.' Look of total contempt. End of story.

And it was the end of the story. My sister phoned long distance, in tearful distress. 'Blackie's d-d-dead!' Me: 'Oh no! What did you . . .' She: 'I wrapped him in red silk and put him in the f-f-freezer, so you could b-b-bury him yourself when you get back!' She was living in a house with several roommates, and I had a vision of one of them pawing through the freezer in search of hamburger and coming across an initially promising packet. Unwrapping of freezer paper. What's this? The Mummy Walks! Eeeking, dropping of frozen cat, flight . . . But that never happened.

We concealed Blackie's death from our daughter for several weeks – she was at university, she was writing exams, it would be upsetting for her – and then we got hell for it.

'How could you *do* this to me? Next time you have to tell me *immediately!*' We came to realize that what she was really afraid of was that one of us would develop a terminal illness, and expire, and possibly be stowed in the freezer, and she wouldn't be informed until it was too late. A parent who has behaved so duplicitously in the matter of a dead cat can surely not be trusted.

I wrote several commemorative poems. I also re-wrote Tennyson's *Morte d'Arthur*, substituting cats. Blackie is the dying king, Sir Cativere is his trusty friend, the three queens on the barge bearing King Blackie to the mouse-filled island orchard of Avilion caterwaul in grief ('And on the mere the mewing died away . . .'). Yes, I know, it was crazed. But strangely therapeutic.

Fluffy followed Blackie shortly after, but in a different way. She developed cat dementia; she could not remember where she was, and would roam the house at night emitting ghostly yowls. She could also not remember what cats were supposed to eat, and would take bites out of strange items. Is it pears? No. What about tomatoes? Not them either. Howl of despair.

But more time has passed. After a long period of

abstinence, during which I told myself that I should not have cats again as I myself was getting a bit older and might trip on them going down the stairs, I have put myself on a list for two Siberian kittens. (Yes, like many cat people I have always had a slight allergy; but this kind of cat is supposed to be low on the allergen scale.) These will be indoor cats, and trained to walk on a leash, or so I fondly believe. Perhaps I will erect a Catio, so they can sunbathe while watching wildlife safely. I will have cat hammocks. I will have scratching posts. I will not allow myself to be distressed by shredded upholstery.

If I'm going to be a mad old lady with a witchy reputation I may as well equip myself with a couple of trusted familiars. Company as one flies through the air on one's broom, wouldn't you say?

TOVE JANSSON

– *from* The Summer Book (1972) –

Translated from the Swedish by Thomas Teal

Finnish writer Tove Jansson (1914–2001) is most widely known as the author of the Moomin books, but she also wrote novels for adults. *The Summer Book* centres on the relationship between six-year-old Sophia and her grandmother as they spend a summer on an island in the Gulf of Finland. Written without embellishments or sentimentality, Jansson's book examines the magic of nature – both in its beauty and violence – and the meaningful bond between a young child and an elderly grandmother; a life just beginning and one nearing the end.

I t was a tiny kitten when it came and could drink its milk only from a nipple. Fortunately, they still had Sophia's baby bottle in the attic. In the beginning, the kitten slept in a tea-cosy to keep warm, but when it found its legs they let it sleep in the cottage in Sophia's bed. It had its own pillow, next to hers.

It was a fisherman's cat and it grew fast. One day, it left the cottage and moved into the house, where it spent its nights under the bed in the box where they kept the dirty dishes. It had odd ideas of its own even then. Sophia carried the cat back to the cottage and tried as hard as she could to ingratiate herself, but the more love she gave it, the quicker it fled back to the dish box. When the box got too full, the cat would howl and someone would have to wash the dishes. Its name was *Ma Petite*, but they called it Moppy.

'It's funny about love,' Sophia said. 'The more you love someone, the less he likes you back.'

'That's very true,' Grandmother observed. 'And so what do you do?'

'You go on loving,' said Sophia threateningly. 'You love harder and harder.'

Her grandmother sighed and said nothing. Moppy was carried around to all the pleasant places a cat might like, but he only glanced at them and walked away. He was flattened with hugs, endured them politely and climbed back into the dish box. He was entrusted with burning secrets and merely averted his yellow gaze. Nothing in the world seemed to interest this cat but food and sleep.

'You know,' Sophia said, 'sometimes I think I hate Moppy. I don't have the strength to go on loving him, but I think about him all the time!'

Week after week, Sophia pursued the cat. She spoke softly and gave him comfort and understanding, and only a couple of times did she lose her patience and yell at him, or pull his tail. At such times Moppy would hiss and run under the house, and afterwards his appetite was better and he slept even longer than usual, curled up in unapproachable softness with one paw daintily across his nose. Sophia stopped playing and started having nightmares. She couldn't think about anything but this cat who refused to be affectionate. Meanwhile Moppy grew into a lean and wild little animal, and one June night he didn't come back to his dish box. In the morning, he walked into the house and stretched – front legs first, with his rear end up in the air – then he closed his eyes and sharpened his claws on the rocking chair, after which he jumped up on the bed and went to sleep. The cat's whole being radiated calm superiority.

He's started hunting, Grandmother thought.

She was right. The very next morning, the cat came in and placed a small dusky yellow bird on the doorstep. Its neck had been deftly broken with one bite, and some bright red drops of blood lay prettily on the shiny coat of feathers. Sophia turned pale and stared fixedly at the murdered bird. She sidled past Moppy, the murderer, with small, forced steps, and then turned and rushed out. Later, Grandmother remarked on the curious fact that wild animals, cats for example, cannot understand the difference between a rat and a bird.

'Then they're dumb!' said Sophia curtly. 'Rats are hideous and birds are nice. I don't think I'll talk to Moppy for three days.' And she stopped talking to her cat.

Every night, the cat went into the woods, and

every morning it killed its prey and carried it into the house to be admired, and every morning the bird was thrown into the sea. A little while later, Sophia would appear outside the window and shout, 'Can I come in? Have you taken out the body?' She punished Moppy and increased her own pain by means of a terrible coarseness. 'Have you cleaned up the blood?' she would yell, or, 'How many murdered today?' And morning coffee was no longer what it had been.

It was a great relief when Moppy finally learned to conceal his crimes. It is one thing to see a pool of blood and quite another thing only to know about it. Moppy probably grew tired of all the screaming and fussing, and perhaps he thought the family ate his birds. One morning when Grandmother was taking her first cigarette on the veranda, she dropped her holder and it rolled through a crack in the floor. She managed to raise one of the planks, and there was Moppy's handiwork – a row of small bird skeletons, all picked clean. Of course she knew that the cat had continued to hunt, and could not have stopped, but the next time he rubbed against her leg as he passed, she drew away and whispered, 'You sly bastard.' The cat dish stood untouched by the steps, and attracted flies.

'You know what?' Sophia said. 'I wish Moppy had never been born. Or else that I'd never been born. That would have been better.'

'So you're still not speaking to each other?' Grandmother asked. 'Not a word,' Sophia said. 'I don't know what to do. And what if I do forgive him – what fun is that when he doesn't even care?' Grandmother couldn't think of anything to say.

Moppy turned wild and rarely came into the house. He was the same colour as the island – a light yellowish grey with striped shadings like granite, or like sunlight on a sand bottom. When he slipped across the meadow by the beach, his progress was like a stroke of wind through the grass. He would watch for hours in the thicket, a motionless silhouette, two pointed ears against the sunset, and then suddenly vanish…and some bird would chirp, just once. He would slink under the creeping pines, soaked by the rain and lean as a streak, and he would wash himself voluptuously when the sun came out. He was an absolutely happy cat, but he didn't share anything with anyone. On hot days, he would roll on the smooth rock, and sometimes he would eat grass and calmly vomit his own hair the way cats do. And what he did between times no one knew.

One Saturday, the Övergårds came for coffee. Sophia went down to look at their boat. It was big, full of bags and jerry cans and baskets, and in one of the baskets a cat was meowing. Sophia lifted the lid and the cat licked her hand. It was a big white cat with a broad face. It kept right on purring when she picked it up and carried it ashore.

'So you found the cat,' said Anna Övergård. 'It's a nice cat, but it's not a mouser, so we thought we'd give it to some friends.'

Sophia sat on the bed with the heavy cat on her lap. It never stopped purring. It was soft and warm and submissive.

They struck a bargain easily, with a bottle of rum to close the deal. Moppy was captured and never knew what was happening until the Övergårds' boat was on its way to town.

The new cat's name was Fluff. It ate fish and liked to be petted. It moved into Sophia's cottage and slept every night in her arms, and every morning it came in to morning coffee and slept some more in the bed beside the stove. If the sun was shining, it would roll on the warm granite.

'Not there!' Sophia yelled. 'That's Moppy's place!' She carried the cat a little farther off, and it licked her on the nose and rolled obediently in the new spot.

The summer grew prettier and prettier, a long series of calm blue summer days. Every night, Fluff slept against Sophia's cheek.

'It's funny about me,' Sophia said. 'I think nice weather gets to be boring.'

'Do you?' her grandmother said. 'Then you're just like your grandfather, he liked storms too.' But before she could say anything else about Grandfather, Sophia was gone.

And gradually the wind came up, sometime during the night, and by morning there was a regular southwester spitting foam all over the rocks.

'Wake up,' Sophia whispered. 'Wake up, kitty, precious, there's a storm.'

Fluff purred and stretched warm sleepy legs in all directions. The sheet was covered with cat hair.

'Get up!' Sophia shouted. 'It's a storm!' But the cat just turned over on its broad stomach. And suddenly Sophia was furious. She kicked open the door and threw the cat out in the wind and watched how it laid its ears back, and she screamed, 'Hunt! Do something! Be like a cat!' And then she started to cry and ran to the guest room and banged on the door.

'What's wrong now?' Grandmother said.

'I want Moppy back!' Sophia screamed.

'But you know how it'll be,' Grandmother said.

'It'll be awful,' said Sophia gravely. 'But it's Moppy I love.'

And so they exchanged cats again.

HILAIRE BELLOC

– *from* A Conversation with a Cat, and Others (1931) –

Hilaire Belloc (1870–1953) was an extremely prolific British-French writer and historian who was also well-known for his religious poetry and his humorous – and moralistic – verses for children. He also wrote widely about fantastic beasts, but in this essay, he recounts a chance meeting with an ordinary cat who charms him out of his solitary and reflective state.

The other day I went into the bar of a railway station and, taking a glass of beer, I sat down at a little table by myself to meditate upon the necessary but tragic isolation of the human soul. I began my meditation by consoling myself with the truth that something in common runs through all nature, but I went on to consider that this cut no ice, and that the heart needed something more. I might by long research have discovered some third term a little less hackneyed than these two, when fate, or some fostering star, sent me a tawny, silky, long-haired cat.

If it be true that nations have the cats they deserve, then the English people deserve well in cats, for there are none so prosperous or so friendly in the world. But even for an English cat this cat was exceptionally friendly and fine – especially friendly. It leapt at one graceful bound into my lap, nestled there, put out an engaging right front paw to touch my arm with a pretty timidity by way of introduction, rolled up at me an eye of bright but innocent affection, and then smiled a secret smile of approval.

No man could be so timid after such an approach as not to make some manner of response. So did I. I even took the liberty of stroking Amathea (for by that name did I receive this vision), and though I began this gesture in a respectful fashion, after the best models of polite deportment with strangers, I was soon lending it some warmth, for I was touched to find that I had a friend; yes, even here, at the ends of the tubes in SW99 [*sic*]. I proceeded (as is right) from caress to speech, and said, 'Amathea, most beautiful of cats, why have you deigned to single me out for so much favour? Did you recognise in me a friend to all that breathes; or were you yourself suffering from loneliness (though I take it you are near your own dear home); or is there pity in the hearts of animals as there is in the hearts of some humans? What, then, was your motive? Or am I, indeed, foolish to ask, and not rather to take whatever good comes to me in whatever way from the gods?'

To these questions Amathea answered with a loud purring noise, expressing with closed eyes of ecstasy her delight in the encounter.

'I am more than flattered, Amathea,' said I, by way of answer, 'I am consoled. I did not know that there was in the world anything breathing and moving, let alone so tawny-perfect, who would give companionship for its own sake and seek out, through deep feeling, some one companion out of all living kind. If you do not address me in words, I know the reason and I commend it; for in words lie the seeds of all dissension and love at its most profound is silent. At least, I read that in a book, Amathea; yes, only the other day. But I confess that the book told me nothing of those gestures which are better than words, or of that caress which I continue to bestow upon you with all the gratitude of my poor heart.'

To this Amathea made a slight gesture of acknowledgement – not disdainful – wagging her head a little and then settling it down in deep content.

'Oh, beautiful-haired Amathea, many have praised you before you found me to praise you, and many will praise you, some in your own tongue, when I am no longer held in the bonds of your presence. But none will praise you more sincerely. For there is not a man living who knows better than I that the four charms of a cat lie in its closed eyes, its long and lovely hair, its silence and even its affected love.'

But at the word 'affected' Amathea raised her head, looked up at me tenderly, once more put forth her paw to touch my arm, and then settled down again to a purring beatitude.

'You are secure,' said I sadly, 'mortality is not before you. There is in your complacency no fore-knowledge of death nor even of separation. And for that reason, Cat, I welcome you the more. For if there has been given to your kind this repose in common living, why, then we men also may find it by following your example and not considering too much what may be to come, and not remembering too much what has been and will never return. Also, I thank you, for this, Amathea, my sweet *Euploka-mos*' (for I was becoming a little familiar through an acquaintance of a full five minutes and from the absence of all recalcitrance), 'that you have reminded me of my youth, and in a sort of shad-owy way, a momentary way, have restored it to me. For there is an age, a blessed youthful age (O my Cat) even with the miserable race of men, when all things are consonant with the life of the body, when sleep is regular and long and deep, when enmities are either unknown or a subject for rejoicing and when the whole of being is lapped in hope as you are now lapped on my lap, Amathea. Yes, we also, we of the doomed race know peace. But whereas you possess it from blind kittenhood to that last dark day so mercifully short with you, we grasp it only for a very little while. But I would not sadden you by the mortal plaint. That would be treason indeed and a vile return for your goodness. What? When you have chosen me out of seven London millions upon whom to confer the tender solace of the heart, when you have proclaimed yourself so suddenly to be my dear, shall I introduce you to the sufferings of those of whom you know nothing save that they feed you, house you, and pass you by? At least you do not take us for gods, as do the dogs, and the more am I humbly beholden to you for this little service of recognition – and something more.'

Amathea slowly raised herself upon her four feet, arched her back, yawned, looked up at me with a smile sweeter than ever and then went round and round, preparing for herself a new couch upon my coat, whereon she settled and began once more to purr in settled ecstasy.

Already had I made sure that a rooted and anchored affection had come to me from out the emptiness and nothingness of the world, and was to feed my soul henceforward; already had I changed the mood of long years and felt a conversion towards the life of things, an appreciation, a cousinship with the created light – and all that through one new link of loving kindness – when, whatever it is that dashes the cup of bliss from the tips of mortal man (Tupper), up and dashed it good and hard. It was the Ancient Enemy who put the fatal sentence into my heart, for we are the playthings of the greater powers and surely some of them are evil.

'You will never leave me, Amathea,' I said. 'I will respect your sleep and we will sit here together through all uncounted time, I holding you in my arms and you dreaming of the fields of Paradise. Nor shall anything part us, Amathea; you are my cat and I am your human. Now and onwards into the fullness of peace.'

Then it was that Amathea lifted herself once more, and with delicate, discreet, unweighted movement of perfect limbs leapt tightly to the floor as lovely as a wave. She walked slowly away from me without so much as looking back over her shoulder. She had another purpose in her mind; and as she so gracefully and so majestically neared the door which she was seeking, a short, unpleasant man standing at the bar said, 'Puss, Puss, Puss!' and stooped to scratch her gently behind the ear. With what a wealth of singular affection, pure and profound, did she not gaze up at him, and then rub herself against his leg in token and external expression of a sacramental friendship that should never die.

– Pangur Bán (The Monk and his Cat), 9th century –

Translated from the Old Irish by W. H. Auden (1954)

Pangur Bán is probably the most famous surviving poem from Early Ireland. Composed by an Irish monk sometime around the 9th century AD, the text compares the scholar's work with the activities of a pet cat, *Pangur Bán*. *The Monk and his Cat* is the title of poet W. H. Auden's 1954 translation.

P angur, white Pangur, How happy we are
    Alone together, scholar and cat
Each has his own work to do daily;
For you it is hunting, for me study.
Your shining eye watches the wall;
My feeble eye is fixed on a book.
You rejoice, when your claws entrap a mouse;
I rejoice when my mind fathoms a problem.
Pleased with his own art, neither hinders the other;
Thus we live ever without tedium and envy.

– *from* The Freud Journal of Lou Andreas-Salomé (1913) –

Translated from the German by Stanley A. Leavy (1964)

Lou Andreas-Salomé was a celebrated Russian-German novelist, poet, essayist and psychoanalyst. Written between 1912–1913, *The Freud Journal* recounts some of her interactions with major figures in contemporary philosophical, literary, and psychoanalytical circles. A diary entry from 2 February 1913, which she titled: 'A Visit to Freud: The Narcissistic Cat – Psychoanalysis as a Gift', describes a visit to Sigmund Freud's house where he talked about various encounters he had had with a cat, a relationship which neatly illustrated one of his theories on the nature of narcissism.

S pent Sunday afternoon until evening at Freud's. This time much more personal conversation, during which he told me of his life, and I promised to bring photographs next time. Most personal of all perhaps was his charming account of the 'narcissistic cat'. While Freud maintained his office on the ground floor, the cat had climbed in through the open window. He did not care much for cats or dogs or animals generally, and in the beginning the cat aroused mixed feelings in him, especially when it climbed down from the sofa on which it had made itself comfortable and began to inspect in passing the antique objects which he had placed for the time being on the floor. He was afraid that by chasing it away he might cause it to move recklessly in the midst of these precious treasures of his. But when the cat proceeded to make known its archaeological satisfaction by purring and with its lithe grace did not cause the slightest damage, Freud's heart melted and he ordered milk for it. From then on the cat claimed its rights daily to take a place on the sofa, inspect the antiques, and get its bowl of milk. However, despite Freud's increasing affection and admiration, the cat paid him not a bit of attention and coldly turned its green eyes with their slanting pupils towards him as toward any other object. When for an instant he wanted more of the cat than its egoistic-narcissistic purring, he had to put his foot down from his comfortable chaise and court its attention with the ingenious enticement of his shoe-toe. Finally, after this unequal relationship had lasted a long time without change, one day he found the cat feverish and gasping on the sofa. And although it was most painstakingly treated with hot fomentations and other remedies, it succumbed to pneumonia, leaving naught of itself but a symbolic picture of all the peaceful and playful charm of true egoism.

ERNEST HEMINGWAY

– Letter to Hadley Mowrer,
25 November 1943 –

Ernest Hemingway (1899–1961) was an American novelist, journalist and sportsman whose understated style
had a strong influence on twentieth-century fiction. He
was married four times and remained close to his first
wife, Hadley Mowrer (with whom he had a son, nick-
named 'Bumby') all his life. In addition to his great fondness for women and drink, Hemingway also loved cats.
In this touching letter, written from his home in Havana,
Finca Vigía, he tells Mowrer about his many cats, the
descendants of which (legend has it) now live at his for-
mer home in Key West, Florida.

Dearest Hadley: Bumby wrote me (first letter
in almost three months and was sure he had
gone over-seas) that you were in the hospital. So has-
ten to write to hope it doesn't amount to anything
and whether it does or not to send much love and
that you be fine soon. Poor Cat I hate to think of
you as ever ill with anything. Hope *so* you are all
right now. This letter brings much, much love and
get well quickness.

Enclosed check is for the money you advanced
for Bumby to come down here when he had his
leave. I felt terribly selfish haveing him but figured
you had seen him in Michigan at the Fort and he

loves this damned place so much and it represents romance, gayety (mis-spelled) and I always load him up with so much good advice and frozen daiquiris that it is probably good for him. I would have sent the check before but have been in and out and over-busy and so lonesome when would get back here without Marty (she's in London for Colliers. Took job when it looked as though I had to be gone three solid months and then I've been stuck here alone half the time) that when come in have a few drinks with my cats and the next thing am asleep on the floor with the Capeheart still playing and all cor-respondence just stacked in two big wooden boxes.

In case you are in hospital or in bed and want to be amused or informed, let's say, there are eleven cats here. One cat just leads to another. The mother is Tester a Persian from the Silver Dawn Cattery somewhere in Florida. She had a kitten named Thruster out of Dillinger a black and white cat from Cojimar a coastal fishing village. By the same sire she also bore Furhouse, Fats, Friendless and Friend-less's Brother. All in the same litter. Two lovely black Persian appearings and two Black and Whites like Dingie. We also have a grey, sort of snow leopard cat named Uncle Wolfer (Persian) and a Tiger cat from Guanabacoa named Good Will after Nelson Rockerfeller. There are at present two half grown kittens named Blindie (on acct. of Blindness. Born that way) daughter of Thruster and her own father.

That shows us eh fat lady? And Nuisance Value also known as Littless Kitty who is the most beautiful of all with a purr-purr that would blast you out of the hospital.

The place is so damned big it doesn't really seem as though there were many cats until you see them all moving like a mass migration at feeding time.

We also have 5 dogs; one good pointer and the others small mongrels on the style of Wax Puppy.

It is wonderful when Marty and/or the kids are here but it is lonesome as a bastard when I'm here alone. I have taught Uncle Wolfer, Dillinger and Will to walk along the railings to the top of the porch pillars and make a pyramid like lions and have taught Friendless to drink with me (Whisky and milk) but even that doesn't take the place of a wife and family.

I never had so damned much time to think in my life, especially nights on the water and here when I can't sleep from haveing lost the habit, and have thought about you with great pleasure and admiration and how wonderful you were and are. Did you ever see anything handsomer than that Bumby after the army had knocked the college fat off of him?

Since I've spent so much time with my cats and seen everything they have to go through I don't mind so much never haveing had a daughter. Marry in heat and repent at leisure was one thing thought up on the boat the other day and the other was something about Custody that great proof of chastity. Maybe

20

I'll turn out to be the Henry James of the People or the comic strips.

So long my dearest Katherine Kat. Paul can't mind me still loveing you because knowing you he would know I would be crazy if I didn't and I have been crazy but never stay that way for very long.

When it is really rough on ocean sing old songs like Oh My Gentlemen, If you've Got Any Feather-Cats, and a Feather Kitty's Talent Lies, the Basque crew think these are folk songs of my Pais [country].

So they are. So, My Pais, get well quickly and take care of yourself and of Paul and accept the obedient devotion of your

Taty

– *from* Making the Cat Laugh: One Woman's Journal of Single Life on the Margins (1996) –

Lynne Truss is an English journalist, novelist and broadcaster best known for her championing of correctness and aesthetics in the English language in *Eats, Shoots & Leaves: The Zero Tolerance Approach to Punctuation*. In this extract from Truss's selected journalism, her uphill (and failed) battle of trying to make her cat laugh over a period of many years is documented with verve.

No Valentines from the cats again. Sometimes I wonder whether they are working as hard at this relationship as I am. Few other pets, I imagine, were lucky enough to find their Valentine's day breakfasts laid out on heart shaped trays, with the words 'From Guess Who' artfully arranged in Kitbits around the edge. But what do I get in return? Not even a single rose. Not even a 'Charming thought, dear. Must rush.' Just the usual unceremonious leap through the cat-flap; the usual glimpse of the flourished furry backside, with its 'Eat my shorts' connotation. Wearily I sweep up the Kitbits with a dustpan and brush, and try to remember whether King Lear was talking about pets when he coined the phrase about the serpent's tooth. Of course, the world would be a distinctly different place if cats suddenly comprehended the concept of give and take – if every time you struggled home with a hundredweight of cat food and said accusingly, 'This is all for you, you know,' the kitties accordingly hung their heads and felt embarrassed. Imagine the scene on the garden wall: 'Honestly, guys, I'd love to come out. But the old lady gave me Sheba this morning, and I kind of feel obligated to stay home.' 'She gave you Sheba?' 'Yeah. But don't go on about it. I feel bad enough that I can never remember to wipe my feet when I come in from the garden. When I think of how much she does for me . . .' (breaks down in sobs). Instead, one takes one's thanks in other ways. For example, take the Valentine's present I bought them: a new cat-nip toy, shaped like a stick of dynamite. This has gone down gratifyingly well, even though the joke misfired slightly. You see, I had fancied the idea of a cat streaking through doorways with a stick of dynamite between its jaws, looking as though it had heroically dived into a threatened mine-shaft and recovered the explosive just in time to save countless lives. In this Lassie Come Home fantasy, however, I was disappointed. Instead, cat number one reacted to the dynamite by drooling an alarming quantity of gooey stuff all over it (as though producing ectoplasm), and then hugging it to his chest and trying to kick it to death with his back paws.

Yet all is not lost. If the cat chooses to reject the heroic image, I can still make the best of it. With a few subtle adjustments to my original plan, I can now play a highly amusing game with the other cat which involves shouting, 'Quick! Take cover! Buster's got a stick of dynamite, and we'll all be blown sky high!' And I dive behind the sofa.

I suppose all this gratitude stuff has been brought to mind because I recently purchased a very expensive cat accessory, which has somehow failed to elicit huzzahs of appreciation. In fact, it has been completely cold shouldered. Called a 'cat's cradle', it is a special fleecy-covered cat-hammock which hooks on to a radiator. The cat is suspended in a cocoon of warmth. A brilliant invention, you might think. Any rational cat would jump straight into it. Too stupid to appreciate the full glory of my gift, however, my own cats sleep underneath it (as though it shelters them from rain), and I begin to lose patience.

'Come on, kitties,' I trilled (at first). 'Mmmm,' I rubbed my cheek on the fleecy stuff. 'Isn't this lovely? Wouldn't this make you feel like a – well, er, like an Eastern potentate, or a genie on a magic carpet, or a very fortunate cat having a nice lie-down suspended from a radiator?' However, I stopped this approach after a week of failure. Now I pull on my thick gardening gloves, grab a wriggling cat by the waist, and hold it firmly on its new bed for about forty-five seconds until it breaks away.

I am reminded of a rather inadequate thing that men sometimes say to women, in an attempt to reassure them. The woman says, 'I never know if you love me, Jonathan,' and the man replies smoothly, 'Well, I'm here, aren't I?' The sub-text to this corny evasion (which fools nobody) is a very interesting cheat – it suggests that, should the slightest thing be wrong with this man's affections, he would of course push off immediately into the wintry night, rather than spend another minute compromising his integrity at the nice fireside with cups of tea.

Having a cat, I find, makes you susceptible to this line of reasoning – perhaps because it is your only direct line of consolation. 'I wonder if he loves me,' you think occasionally (perhaps as you search the doormat in vain for Valentines with paw-prints on them). And then you gently lift the can-opener from its velvet cushion in the soundproofed kitchen, and with a loud kerchunk-chunk a cat comes cannoning through the cat-flap, and skids backwards across the lino on its bum. And you think cheerfully, 'Well, of course he does. I mean, he's here, isn't he?'

LEWIS CARROLL

– *from* Alice's Adventures in Wonderland (1865) –

Charles Lutwidge Dodgson (1832–1898), better known by his pen name Lewis Carroll, was a mathematician, photographer, inventor, Anglican deacon and writer, most notably of *Alice's Adventures in Wonderland* and its sequel *Through the Looking-Glass*. In 'Alice meets the Cheshire Cat', we come across what is arguably the most famous grin in literature.

A lice was just beginning to think to herself, 'Now, what am I to do with this creature when I get it home?' when it grunted again, so violently, that she looked down into its face in some alarm. This time there could be *no* mistake about it: it was neither more nor less than a pig, and she felt that it would be quite absurd for her to carry it further.

So she set the little creature down, and felt quite relieved to see it trot away quietly into the wood. 'If it had grown up,' she said to herself, 'it would have made a dreadfully ugly child: but it makes rather a handsome pig, I think.' And she began thinking over other children she knew, who might do very well as pigs, and was just saying to herself, 'if one only knew the right way to change them –' when she was a little startled by seeing the Cheshire Cat sitting on a bough of a tree a few yards off.

The Cat only grinned when it saw Alice. It looked good-natured, she thought: still it had *very* long claws and a great many teeth, so she felt that it ought to be treated with respect.

'Cheshire Puss,' she began, rather timidly, as she did not at all know whether it would like the name: however, it only grinned a little wider. 'Come, it's pleased so far,' thought Alice, and she went on. 'Would you tell me, please, which way I ought to go from here?'

'That depends a good deal on where you want to get to,' said the Cat.

'I don't much care where –' said Alice.

'Then it doesn't matter which way you go,' said the Cat.

'– so long as I get *somewhere*,' Alice added as an explanation.

'Oh, you're sure to do that,' said the Cat, 'if you only walk long enough.'

Alice felt that this could not be denied, so she tried another question. 'What sort of people live about here?'

'In *that* direction,' the Cat said, waving its right paw round, 'lives a Hatter: and in *that* direction,' waving the other paw, 'lives a March Hare. Visit either you like: they're both mad.'

'But I don't want to go among mad people,' Alice remarked.

'Oh, you can't help that,' said the Cat: 'we're all mad here. I'm mad. You're mad.'

'How do you know I'm mad?' said Alice.

'You must be,' said the Cat, 'or you wouldn't have come here.'

Alice didn't think that proved it at all; however, she went on 'And how do you know that you're mad?'

'To begin with,' said the Cat, 'a dog's not mad. You grant that?'

'I suppose so,' said Alice.

'Well, then,' the Cat went on, 'you see, a dog growls when it's angry, and wags its tail when it's pleased. Now I growl when I'm pleased and wag my tail when I'm angry. Therefore, I'm mad.'

'I call it purring, not growling,' said Alice.

'Call it what you like,' said the Cat. 'Do you play croquet with the Queen today?'

'I should like it very much,' said Alice, 'but I haven't been invited yet.'

'You'll see me there,' said the Cat, and vanished.

Alice was not much surprised at this; she was getting so used to queer things happening.

While she was looking at the place where it had been, it suddenly appeared again.

'By-the-bye, what became of the baby?' said the Cat. 'I'd nearly forgotten to ask.'

'It turned into a pig,' Alice quietly said, just as if it had come back in a natural way.

'I thought it would,' said the Cat, and vanished again.

Alice waited a little, half expecting to see it again, but it did not appear, and after a minute or two she walked on in the direction in which the March Hare was said to live. 'I've seen hatters before,' she said to herself; 'the March Hare will be much the most interesting, and perhaps as this is May it won't be raving mad – at least not so mad as it was in March.' As she said this, she looked up, and there was the Cat again, sitting on a branch of a tree.

'Did you say pig, or fig?' said the Cat.

'I said pig,' replied Alice; 'and I wish you wouldn't keep appearing and vanishing so suddenly: you make one quite giddy.'

'All right,' said the Cat; and this time it vanished quite slowly, beginning with the end of the tail, and ending with the grin, which remained some time after the rest of it had gone.

'Well! I've often seen a cat without a grin,' thought Alice; 'but a grin without a cat! It's the most curious thing I ever saw in my life!'

DORIS LESSING

– *from* Particularly Cats (1967) –

Doris May Lessing (1919–2013) was born to British parents in Iran, where she lived until 1925. She is the author of over fifty books and was awarded the Nobel Prize for Literature in 2007. Her connection with cats began during her childhood in Southern Rhodesia (now Zimbabwe), where both wild cats and working mousers roamed her family's farmstead. Later she was drawn to the softer, more domestic cats who came to share her life in various London flats.

In the middle of that winter, friends were offered a kitten. Friends of theirs had a Siamese cat, and she had a litter by a street cat. The hybrid kittens were being given away. Their flat is minute, and they both worked all day; but when they saw the kitten, they could not resist. During its first weekend it was fed on tinned lobster soup and chicken mousse, and it disrupted their much-married nights because it had to sleep under the chin, or at least, somewhere against the flesh, of H, the man. S, his wife, announced on the telephone that she was losing the affections of her husband to a cat, just like the wife in Colette's tale. On Monday they went off to work leaving the kitten by itself, and when they came home it was crying and sad, having been alone all day. They said they were bringing it to us. They did.

The kitten was six weeks old. It was enchanting, a delicate fairytale cat, whose Siamese genes showed in the shape of the face, ears, tail, and the subtle lines of its body. Her back was tabby: from above or the back, she was a pretty tabby kitten, in grey and cream. But her front and stomach were a smoky-gold, Siamese cream, with half-bars of black at the neck. Her face was pencilled with black – fine dark rings around the eyes, fine dark streaks on her cheeks, a tiny cream-coloured nose with a pink tip, outlined in black. From the front, sitting with her slender paws straight, she was an exotically beautiful beast. She sat, a tiny thing, in the middle of a yellow carpet, surrounded by five worshippers, not at all afraid of us. Then she stalked around that floor of the house, inspecting every inch of it, climbed upon to my bed, crept under the fold of a sheet, and was at home.

S went off with H saying: Not a moment too soon, otherwise I wouldn't have a husband at all.

And he went off groaning, saying that nothing could be as exquisite as being woken by the delicate touch of a pink tongue on his face.

The kitten went, or rather hopped, down the stairs, each of which was twice her height: first front paws, then flop, with the back; front paws, then flop with the back. She inspected the ground floor, refused the tinned food offered to her, and demanded a dirt box by mewing for it. She rejected wood shavings, but torn newspaper was acceptable, so her fastidious pose said, if there was nothing else. There wasn't: the earth outside was frozen solid.

She would not eat tinned cat food. She would not. And I was not going to feed her lobster soup and chicken. We compromised on some minced beef.

She had always been as fussy over her food as a bachelor gourmet. She gets worse as she gets older. Even as a kitten she could express annoyance, or pleasure, or a determination to sulk, by what she ate, half-ate, or chose to refuse. Her food habits are an eloquent language.

But I think it is just possible she was taken away from her mother too young. If I might respectfully suggest it to the cat experts, it is possible they are wrong when they say a kitten may leave its mother the day it turns six weeks old. This cat was six weeks, not a day more, when it was taken from its other. The basis of her dandyism over food is the neurotic hostility and suspicion towards it of a child with food problems. She had to eat, she supposed; she did eat; but she has never eaten with enjoyment, for the sake of eating. And she shares another characteristic with people who have not had enough mother-warmth. Even now she will instinctively creep under the fold of a newspaper, or into a box or a basket – anything that shelters, anything that covers. More; she is over ready to see insult; over ready to sulk. And she is a frightful coward.

Kittens who are left with their mother seven or eight weeks eat easily, and they have confidence. But of course, they are not as interesting.

As a kitten, this cat never slept on the outside of the bed. She waited until I was in it, then she walked all over me, considering possibilities. She would get right down into the bed, by my feet, or on to my shoulder, or crept under the pillow. If I moved too much, she huffily changed quarters, making her annoyance felt.

When I was making the bed, she was happy to be made into it; and stayed, visible as a tiny lump, quite happily, sometimes for hours, between the blankets. If you stroked the lump, it purred and mewed. But she would not come out until she had to.

The lump would move across the bed, hesitate at the edge. There might be a frantic mew as she slid to the floor. Dignity disturbed, she licked herself hastily, glaring yellow eyes at the viewers, who made a mistake if they laughed. Then, every hair conscious of itself, she walked to some centre stage.

Time for the fastidious pernickety eating. Time for the earth box, as exquisite a performance. Time for setting the creamy fur in order. And time for play, which never took place for its own sake, but only when she was being observed.

She was as arrogantly aware of herself as a pretty girl who has no attributes but her prettiness: body and face always posed according to some inner monitor – a pose which is as good as a mask: no, no, *this* is what I am, the aggressive breasts, the sullen hostile eyes always on the watch for admiration.

Cat, at the age when, if she were human, she would be wearing clothes and hair like weapons, but confident that any time she chose she might relapse into indulged childhood again, because the role had become too much of a burden – cat posed and princessed and preened about the house and then, tired, a little peevish, tucked herself into the fold of a newspaper or behind a cushion, and watched the world safely from there.

Her prettiest trick, used mostly for company, was to lie on her back under a sofa and pull herself along by her paws, in fast sharp rushes, stopping to turn her elegant little head sideways, yellow eyes narrowed, waiting for applause. 'Oh beautiful kitten! Delicious beast! Pretty cat!' Then on she went for another display.

Or, on the right surface, the yellow carpet, a blue cushion, she lay on her back and slowly rolled, paws tucked up, head back, so that her creamy chest and stomach were exposed, marked faintly, as if she were a delicate subspecies of leopard, with black blotches, like the roses of leopards. 'Oh beautiful kitten, oh you are so beautiful.' And she was prepared to go on until the compliments stopped.

Or she sat in the back verandah, not on the table, which was unadorned, but on a little stand that had narcissus and hyacinth in earthenware pots. She sat posed between spikes of blue and white flowers, until she was noticed and admired. Not only by us, of course; also by the old rheumatic tom who prowled, grim reminder of a much harder life, around the garden where the earth was still frost bound. He saw a pretty half-grown cat, behind glass. She saw him. She lifted her head, this way, that way; bit off a fragment of hyacinth, dropped it; licked her fur, negligently; then with an insolent backwards glance, leaped down and came indoors and out of his sight. Or, on the way upstairs, on an arm or a shoulder, she would glance out of the window and see the poor old beast, so still that sometimes we thought he must have died and been frozen there. When the sun warmed a little at midday and he sat licking himself, we were relieved. Sometimes she sat watching him from the window, but her life was still to be tucked into the arms, beds, cushions, and corners of human beings.

Then the spring came, the back door was opened, the dirt box, thank goodness, made unnecessary, and the back garden became her territory. She was six months old, fully grown, from the point of view of nature.

She was so pretty then, so perfect; more beautiful even than that cat who, all those years ago, I swore could never have an equal. Well of course there hasn't been; for that cat's nature was all tact, delicacy, warmth and grace – so, as the fairy tales and the old wives say, she had to die young.

Our cat, the princess, was, still is, beautiful, but, there is no glossing it, she's a selfish beast.

The cats lined up on the garden walls. First, the sombre old winter cat, king of the back gardens. Then, a handsome black-and-white from next door, his son, from the look of it. A battle-scarred tabby. A grey-and-white cat who was so certain of defeat that he never came down from the wall. And a dashing tigerish young tom that she clearly admired. No use, the old king had not been defeated. When she strolled out, tail erect, apparently ignoring them all, but watching the handsome young tiger, he leaped down towards her, but the winter cat had only to stir where he lay on the wall, and the young at jumped back to safety. This went on for weeks.

Meanwhile, H and S came to visit their lost pet. S said how frightful and unfair it was that the princess could not have her choice; and H said that was entirely as it should be: a princess must have a king, even if he was old and ugly. He has such dignity, said H; he has such presence; and he had earned the pretty young cat because of his noble endurance of the long winter.

By then the ugly cat was called Mephistopheles. (In his own home, we heard, he was called Billy.) Our cat had been called various names, but none of them stuck. Melissa and Franny; Marilyn and

Sappho; Circe and Ayesha and Suzette. But in conversation, in love-talk, she miaowed and purred and throated in response to the long drawn-out syllables of adjectives – beee*ooo*ti-ful, de*lic*ious puss.

On a very hot weekend, the only one, I seem to remember, in a nasty summer, she came in heat.

H and S came to lunch on the Sunday, and we sat on the back verandah and watched the choices of nature. Not ours. And not our cat's, either.

For two nights the fighting had gone on, awful fights, cats wailing and howling and screaming in the garden. Meanwhile grey puss had sat on the bottom of my bed, watching into the dark, ears lifting and moving, tail commenting, just slightly at the tip.

On that Sunday, there was only Mephistopheles in sight. Grey cat was rolling in ecstasy all over the garden. She came to us and rolled around our feet and bit them. She rushed up and down the tree at the bottom of the garden. She rolled and cried, and called, and invited.

The most disgraceful exhibition of lust I've ever seen,' said S watching H, who was in love with our cat.

'Oh poor cat,' said H; 'If I were Mephistopheles I'd never treat you so badly.'

'Oh, H,' said S, 'you are disgusting, if I told people they'd never believe it. But I've always said, you're disgusting.'

'So that's what you've always said,' said H, caressing the ecstatic cat.

It was a very hot day, we had a lot of wine for lunch, and the love play went on all afternoon.

Finally, Mephistopheles leaped down off the wall to where grey cat was wriggling and rolling – but alas, he bungled it.

'Oh my God,' said H, genuinely suffering. 'It is really not forgivable, that sort of thing.'

S, anguished, watched the torments of our cat, and doubted, frequently, dramatically and loudly, whether sex was worth it. 'Look at it,' she said, 'that's us. That's what we're like.'

'That's not at all what we're like,' said H. 'It's Mephistopheles. He should be shot'

Shoot him at once, we all said; or at least lock him up so that the young tiger from next door could have his chance.

But the handsome young cat was not visible. We went on drinking wine; the sun went on shining; our princess danced, rolled, rushed up and down the tree, and, when at last things went well, was clipped again and again by the old king.

'All that's wrong,' said H, 'is that he's too old for her.

'Oh my God,' said S, 'I'm going to take you home. Because if I don't, I swear you'll make love to that cat yourself.

'Oh I wish I could,' said H. 'What an exquisite

beast, what a lovely creature, what a princess, she's wasted on a cat, I can't stand it.'

Next day winter returned; the garden was cold and wet; and grey cat had returned to her fastidious disdainful ways. And the old king lay on the garden wall in the slow English rain, still victor of them all, waiting.

– It Looks Bad for the Three Little Lardner Kittens (1922) –

Ringgold Wilmer Lardner (1885–1933), widely known for his sly and often cynical short stories, was also one of the most famous journalists in America during the 1920s and 1930s, with writers such as Ernest Hemingway, John O'Hara, Virginia Woolf and F. Scott Fitzgerald all professing strong admiration for his writing. Often he used sport journalism to talk about politics, Prohibition and war, or to offer his readers acutely observed snapshots of American life.

New York – Amongst the inmates of our heavily mortgaged home in Great Neck is 3 members of what is sometimes referred to as the feline tribe born the 11th day of last April and christened respectully. Barney, Blackie and Ringer. These 3 little ones is motherless, as the lady cat who bore them, aptly named Robin Hood took sick one June day and was give away by Fred to a friend to whom he kindly refrained from mentioning her illness. These 3 little members of the feline tribe is the cutest and best behaved kitties in all catdom. Their conduct having always been above reproaches outside of a tendency on the part of Ringer to bite strangers' knuckles. Nowhere on Long Island is a more loveable trio of grimalkins, and it pierces my old heart to think that some day next week these 3 little fellows must be shot down like a dog so as their fur can be fashioned into warm Winter coat for she who their antics has so often caused to screek with laughter. Yes boys the 3 little kittens is practically doomed you might say and all because today's game at the Polo grounds was not called on account of darkness long before it started though they was no time during the afternoon when the Yanks could see.

I probably never would of heard of a cat skin coat was it not for an accidental introduction last night to a man who has did nothing all his life but sell and wear fur coats and who told me that no finer or more warmer garment can be fashioned than is made from the skin of a milkfed kitty.

'Listen,' was the way he put it, 'you would be a even worse sucker than you are if you was to squander thousands on thousands of dollars on the fur of a muskrat or a mule when you have right in your own asylum the makings of the most satisfactory and handsome coat that money can buy.'

'Yes,' was my reply, 'but the fur of 3 kittens would make a mighty small coat.'

'Small coats is the rage,' was his reply, 'and I personally seen some of the best dressed women in New York strolling up and down 10th avenue during the last cold snap with cat skin garments no bigger than a guest towel.'

So while I said a few paragraphs back that the

result of this ball game spelled the doom of our little kitties, why as a matter of fact I have just about made up my mind to not buy no costly furs even if the Yanks does come through and bring me out on the right side of the public ledger. Whatever I win in bets on this serious I will freely give to charity.

I would try and describe the game to you in intimate detail was it not played in such darkness that I was only able to see a few incidences. One of these occurred in the 3rd inning and consisted of Whitey Witt getting caught asleep off of first base by a snap throw from one of the Smith brothers. Henry Edwards, the dean of Cleveland baseball experts, explained this incidence by saying that Whitey thought he was still with the Athletics. It is more likely however that Whitey was deceived by the darkness into believing it was his bed time.

The next incidence come in the 4th inning when the Babe tried to go from first to third on a wallop by Bob Meusel that got away from Frisch. Frankie pegged the ball to Heine Groh who stood in Babe's path to third but it was so dark that Babe crashed right smack into him and secured a rolling fall. For a minute it looked like they would be fisticuffs between the 2 famous athletes but Heine suddenly remembered the advice given him by his first school teacher, 'Never be a bully,' and the fight was over before it begun.

Fifteen minutes before the start of the game the

official announcer come up to the press box and said that McQuillan was going to pitch for the Giants. A minute later he come around again and said to make it Scott instead of McQuillan. McQuillan thus broke Fred Toney's record for the length of time spent in a world series ball game.

I will close this article by making a apology to the boys to who I have give tickets for games no 1 and 3 and whose seats is in section 24 which is as far north as you can get without falling out of the grandstand. The gents who sold me these seats thought I was a close friend of the Meusel boys and might want to set out there myself and kid with them.

[POSTSCRIPT]

'Yanks Lose, But Lardner Kittens Spared' (1922)

Now boys I suppose they is a few interested in whether the little woman is going to get a costly fur coat. The other day I wrote a story to the general effects that we was going to kill our cats and use their fur to make the costly garment. This story was not apreciated in the heavily mortgaged home. After a long argument the master of the house compromised and decided to not doom the little members of the finny tribe to death. Instead of that we are going to use a idear furnished by the same Eddie Batchelor of Detroit mentioned a few thousand words ago. Eddie's idears is to start a chain letter to all our friends and readers asking them to look around the old homestead and find their family albums and take the plush off of the covers and send it to the undersigned and make a plush coat which everybody tells me is the most fashionable fur on the green footstool. The little woman can wear plush and a specially the red pigment but black and tan plush covers will be welcomed and this man tells me theys nothing more attractive than a black and red and tan blocked coat made out of plush albums.

– Mog the Cat and the Mysteries of Animal Subjectivity (2019) –

Judith Kerr (1923–2019) was a German-born British writer and illustrator whose family fled to Britain in 1935. She is the author of the semi-autobiographical *When Hitler Stole Pink Rabbit* (1971), which gave a child's-eye view of the Second World War, and acclaimed novels for older children, but is perhaps most famous for her children's books about Mog, a 'nice but not very clever' cat. First published in the *New Yorker*, Naomi Fry's essay examines the nature of mutuality and understanding in these classics of children's literature.

'Once there was a cat called Mog. She lived with a family called Thomas. Mog was nice but not very clever. She didn't understand a lot of things. A lot of other things she forgot. She was a very forgetful cat.' So begins Judith Kerr's picture book 'Mog the Forgetful Cat' published in England in 1970.

Though this was only the first of Kerr's 'Mog' volumes – which ended up numbering more than a dozen by the time the last of the bunch, 'Goodbye Mog' came out, in 2002 – these opening lines establish the series' rhythm and sensibility. Kerr, who died in May, at the age of ninety-five, having published more than thirty much beloved books in the course of her career, once said that she tried never to use more than two hundred and fifty words in any of her books, so that young children could follow along. But it was, perhaps, exactly this limitation that heightened her ability to pinpoint, with a beautiful specificity, the character of her feline protagonist. Just like Mog – a stout, friendly tabby with a round face, a white bib, and white paws, who gets into a variety of small domestic scrapes because of her limited grasp of the world around her – Kerr's language is simple and a little plodding. The sentences are short and of consistent length – not unlike the padded footfalls of a rotund cat – and, in their occasional repetitiveness, mimic a feline's clumsy thinking.

Mog could be considered a descendant of A. A. Milne's Pooh, that portly 'Bear of very Little Brain' who says, 'Long words bother me.' But Pooh, though self-professedly dense, is still able to participate in adventures that require elaborate, if often misguided, planning, and is aware, besides, of his own intellectual limitations. Mog is an even simpler creature.

Her needs, like a real-life cat's, are basic – eating, sleeping, snuggling, defecating – and Kerr's books ventriloquise these imperatives in a manner that both admits their humble nature and respects it, portraying an animal subjectivity that for all its plainness is no less particular in its quirks, and no less worthy of our recognition, than that of a more complex creature.

As any feline lover knows, all happy cats are alike, but each unhappy cat is unhappy in its own way, and a certain want of satisfaction is what sets up Mog's narrative in 'Mog the Forgetful Cat'. One morning at the Thomas household – composed of Mr. and Mrs. Thomas and their young children, Debbie and Nicky – Mog wakes up in a foul mood. Nicky picks her up against her will ('Mog said nothing, but she wasn't happy'); she climbs on the breakfast table and tries to eat an egg ('Mog forgot that cats have milk for breakfast'), arousing Mr. Thomas's annoyance ('Bother that cat!'); going outside, she is chased by a dog and, forgetting how to use her cat flap to make it safely back into the house, meows loudly at the kitchen window and scares Mrs. Thomas ('Bother that cat!'); she falls asleep on Mrs. Thomas's hat, crushing it; she hangs her tail over the TV when Mr. Thomas wants to watch it; and, in licking the sleeping Debbie, she makes her have a bad dream. ('The tiger wanted to eat Debbie . . . Debbie shouted. Mog jumped.') Confronted with the family's ire ('Bother, bother, BOTHER that cat!'), Mog escapes to the garden, where she broods: 'She was very sad. The garden was dark. The house was dark too. Mog sat in the dark and thought dark thoughts.'

When I read this line for the first time, to my daughter, it seemed to capture an entirely recognisable mood, both internal and environmental. It was just as pointed, and as poignant, as 'I wear black on the outside / 'Cause black is how I feel on the inside', a lyric written a decade and a half later by the Smiths. Kerr also illustrated the books, and her pictures, like her language, are more expressive for their simplicity. After leaving the house, the broad-faced cat sits among naïvely figured grass and leaves – there is, perhaps, a hint of a Henri Rousseau-like jungle here, with Mog as the domesticated tiger – her perfectly round eyes shining beseechingly, like two yellow and black marbles. A sense of a vivid life, yearning to be understood, is present in every line. 'Nobody likes me,' she thinks. 'They've all gone to bed. There's no one to let me in. And they haven't even given me my supper.' Mog, of course, must have got her supper – she is, as we know, forgetful – but this bit of greedy-pet comedy doesn't detract from the moment's pathos.

The book is not the first of Kerr's to consider the essential failure of communication between man and beast. In Kerr's first and perhaps most famous picture book, 'The Tiger Who Came to Tea' published in 1968, a young girl named Sophie and her mother welcome a bright-orange, friendly but voracious tiger into their flat. The visit is figured as rompish rather than traumatic (and the charac-ters' swinging-sixties outfits – from a purple frock to slim checked pants – add a colourful riotousness to the pages), but there is nonetheless a certain troubling incompatibility between the humans and the tiger. Bounding about from cupboard to fridge, the animal commences to eat all the food in the house and to quaff all the milk from the milk jug, the tea from the teapot, and the water from the tap. But, as soon as the food is gone, he leaves, disappearing into the night. If only the tiger could speak, Sophie and her mummy would know where he came from and where he was going, but the animal reveals nothing. In an effort to secure his return, the family, we are told at the end of the book, buys 'a very big tin of tiger food' at the grocery store to feed the beast 'in case [he] should come to tea again.' 'But,' as the slightly melancholy final line notes, 'he never did.'

If in 'Tiger' Kerr describes miscommunication from the human perspective, the 'Mog' books examine it from that of the animal. For Kerr, the chief problem with being a cat is that your needs often come up against those of an uncomprehending or unwilling world. Often, however, the books rely on such misapprehension not just for their animating conflict but also for their resolution. When a burglar steals into the house in 'Mog the Forgetful Cat' Mog, still sitting in the garden, meows 'her biggest meow, very sudden and very, very loud', hoping that the burglar will let her in through the kitchen window, as the family sometimes does. ('Perhaps he will give me my supper.') The burglar, alarmed, drops his bag, waking the Thomases, who call the police. After the robber is caught, Mog, no longer a bothersome cat, is called 'remarkable' by a policeman, awarded a medal, and given an egg for breakfast.

Other 'Mog' books proceed in a similar fashion. In 'Mog and the Baby' a very reluctant Mog is charged with amusing a friend's grabby tot ('Mog loves babies' Mrs. Thomas confidently promises, a statement undermined by Mog's disapproving moue). When the baby, referred to as 'it' throughout, stumbles out into the street, Mog saves him from a moving car, entirely by chance, and ends up receiving a large fish as a reward. ('She is the bravest cat in the world.' Nicky says.) In 'Mog's Bad Thing' after a tent is erected in the back yard to hold the neighbourhood cat show, obscuring the tree where Mog usually goes to the 'lavatory' she does 'a bad thing' on Mr. Thomas's green chair. She redeems herself, later, when she accidentally falls out of the attic window and into the tent while wrapped in a curtain and manages to win first prize in the contest for her originality ('And in a little dress!'). And so it goes: there is connection and affection, but there will never be full, mutual comprehension.

Anyone who has pets will likely recognise the human impulse to imbue them with thoughts and feelings that they most likely don't have. It's a pathetic fallacy I partake in every day, taking on a sing-song voice to ask my cats why they 'look a little sad today' and wondering if 'watching 'The Real Housewives' with me might help take their minds off things.' Kerr beautifully teases out this tendency: while Mog does have thoughts and feelings, they are rarely the ones that the humans around her think that she does. From this proceeds the broader question of whether, if we can't understand our fellow cat, we can understand our fellow man. In 'Mog the Forgetful Cat' when Debbie awakes, shouting, from her nightmare, her parents rush to her side, but she remains inconsolable and wordless: 'Debbie said nothing. She was still crying because of the bad dream.' Her parents can comfort her, but they can't know her thoughts, just as they can't know Mog's. For better or worse, there is an unbridgeable divide between all of us. The 'Mog' books allow us the momentary pleasure of glimpsing beyond it, but they also remind us that, in the end, we're alone.

MURIEL SPARK

– *from* Robinson (1958) –

Dame Muriel Sarah Spark (1918–2006) was an Edin-
burgh-born writer and poet whose darkly comedic voice
made her one of the most distinctive writers of the twentieth century. Best known for her novel *The Prime of Miss
Jean Brodie* (1961), Spark's second novel, *Robinson*, centres on three survivors of a plane crash who find themselves on a remote island belonging to a recluse called
Robinson. What follows is a surreal tale of manipula-
tion, survival, suspicion and mystery, narrated through
the journal of one of the survivors, who passes the time
teaching Robinson's cat to play ping-pong.

T o teach a cat to play ping-pong you have first
to win the confidence and approval of the
cat. Bluebell was the second cat I had undertaken
to teach; I found her more amenable than the first,
which had been a male.

Ping-pong with a cat is a simplified and more
individualistic form of the proper game. You play it
close to the ground and you imagine the net.

Gaining a cat's confidence is different from
gaining the confidence of any other animal. Food
is not the simple answer. You have to be prepared
to play with it for as long as two hours on end. To
gain the initial interest of a cat, I always place a piece
of paper over my head and face and utter meows

and other cat noises. This is irresistible to most cats, who come nosing up to see what is going on behind the paper. The next phase involves soft whispering alternately with the whistling of high-pitched tunes.

I thought Bluebells of Scotland would be appropriate to Bluebell. She was enchanted. It made her purr and rise on her hind legs to paw my shoulder as I crouched on the patio whistling to her in the early afternoons.

After that I began daily to play with her, sometimes throwing the ping-pong ball in the air. She often leapt beautifully and caught it in her forepaws. By the second week in June I had so far won her confidence and approval as to be able to make fierce growling noises at her. She liked these very much, and would crouch menacingly before me, springing suddenly at me in a mock attack. Sometimes I would stalk her, one slow step after another, bent double, and with glaring eyes. She loved this wildly, making flying leaps at my down-thrust head.

'You'll get a nasty scratch one day,' said Robinson.

'Oh, I understand cats,' I said.

'She understands cats,' said Jimmie unnecessarily. Robinson walked away.

Having worked round Bluebell to a stage where she would let me do nearly anything with her and play rough-house as I pleased, I got an old carton out of Robinson's storehouse and set it on end against the patio wall. Bluebell immediately sat herself inside this little three-walled house. Then the first ping-pong lesson began. I knelt down two yards away from her and placed the ball in front of me. She crouched in readiness as if it were an ordinary ball game. With my middle finger and thumb I pinged the ball into Bluebell's box. It bounced against the walls. The cat sprang at it and batted it back. I sent it over again to Bluebell. This time she caught it in her forepaws and curled up on the ground, biting it and kicking it with her silver hind pads. However, for a first lesson her style was not bad. Within a week Bluebell had got the ping-pong idea. Four times out of ten she would send the ball back to me, sometimes batting it with her hind leg most comically, so that even Miguel had to laugh. On the other occasions she would appropriate the ball for herself, either dribbling it right across the patio, or patting it under her body and then sitting on it. Sometimes she would pat the ball only a little way in front of her, waiting for me, with her huge green eyes, to come and retrieve it.

The cat quickly discovered that the setting up of her carton on the patio was the start of the ping-pong game, and she was always waiting for me at that spot after lunch.

She was an encouraging pupil, an enthusiast. One day when she was doing particularly well, and I was encouraging her with my lion growl to her great excitement, I heard Robinson's voice from the back of the house.

'Bluebell! Pussy-puss Bluebell. Nice puss. Come on!'

Her ear twitched very slightly in response, but she was at the ball and patting it over to me, it seemed in one movement. I cracked it back, and she forth again.

'Bluebell! Where's the cat?' said Robinson, appearing on the patio just as I was growling more. 'There's a mouse in the storehouse. Do you mind?' he said to me.

The cat had her eyes on my hand which held the ball. I picked her up and handed her to Robinson. Bluebell struggled to free herself and go for the ball. I thought this funny and giggled accordingly. But Bluebell was born reluctantly away by solemn Robinson, with Miguel following like a righteous little retainer.

Jimmie grinned. Something about Jimmie's grin and Robinson's bearing embarrassed me. I began to wonder if Robinson felt intensely about incidents like this. I should not myself have thought of the affair as an 'incident' at all. It was a great bore.

EDWARD GOREY

– *from* The Cat on My Shoulder:
Writers and their Cats (1993) –

Edited by Lisa Angowski Rogak

Edward Gorey (1925–2000) was an American writer and
artist noted for his 'gothic' pen-and-ink drawings, which
often depict vaguely unsettling scenes in Victorian and
Edwardian settings, and his timeless illustrations for the
1982 edition of T. S. Eliot's whimsical cat poems, *Old
Possum's Book of Practical Cats.* An animal lover to the
end, Gorey left his estate to a charitable trust benefit-
ing cats and dogs, as well as less precious animals like
bats and insects.

I've always had at least one cat. At the moment I
have seven. I love them dearly, but I sometimes
feel they're largely an irritation, and I seem to spend
most of my time screaming at them not to do things,
not that it does any good. Whenever I read about
people who train their cats not to scratch the furniture, I think, 'Oh, they're very lucky, the cat just
doesn't want to.' In my experience, no matter how
many times I scream at them not to do a particular
thing, they still go ahead and do it.

Occasionally, due to my own carelessness, they'll
ruin a drawing because I'll leave a bottle of ink open
and they'll walk across the paper. I can't leave a pen

lying on the board because even if Thomas is at the other end of the house, he'll know when I walk away from the drawing board even for a split second and will rush in to play with the pens. I'm missing about half a dozen pens.

My two oldest cats are ginger tabs named Billy and Charlie. The next oldest ones are named George and Weedon; then I have a brother and two sisters named Thomas, Alice and Jane. They all get along very well together, and they tend to sleep in one great big lump. There are a couple that sit up on my drawing board while I'm working. They're all such good friends. They almost never hiss at each other, but maybe once or twice a day one will hit another one where I can't see them and I'll yell, 'Stop it! Stop it! Stop it!'

When I lived in New York for part of the year in a one-room apartment, I felt three cats was as much as I could handle, although I did end up with six for a year or two. Let's put it this way, I will probably have acquired a few more by the time this book comes out. I have a couple of cousins who live near me, and occasionally they go off to the ASPCA to get a cat, and I always ask why? Good God, I live in mortal terror of finding more outside, or somebody turning up on my doorstep. With one exception, all of my cats have been strays. People come and say, 'If you don't take this cat, it's going to the pound.' God knows I do that myself. When I've come across a stray and I can't have any more cats, I blackmail people. You know: 'You owe me one, here's a cat, take it.'

They can be the most godawful nuisances. The minute I go to bed, Charlie comes up and claws me because he wants to sleep right in the crook of my arm and his nose in my face. Nothing I can do will stop him. If I put the bedclothes over my head, he'll just sit there clawing at the bedclothes until I finally give up. And, of course, once he's there, he wants to leave after five minutes. So, in the middle of the night he leaves, and then he wants to come back in and he'll start clawing at the bedclothes again. Jane and Thomas both like coming under the bedclothes briefly, but then they slither out again, and they only want to go between part of the bedclothes, under one bedspread and one blanket. Then there's another who wants to go under only two blankets. I have to allow them to weasel their way in, so when all seven have decided they want to sleep in the bed, it's definitely difficult to turn over.

Cats are pretty independent and they go about leading their own lives in the house. I wouldn't live without them. In one way they're very demanding, but in another way they're not demanding at all. My cats have influenced me a great deal, but I can say I have no idea what they're thinking about. None of my cats ever seem to do anything wonderfully picturesque, or wonderfully clever, and nobody's been abysmally stupid, either.

We all sit on the couch and watch television together. They have an annoying tendency to stand up and get in the way of the TV and block the view just at the crucial moment. We watch TV upstairs in a room with skylights and sometimes they'll all suddenly look up at once, and I have no idea what they're seeing. The only time I get spooked living alone is when the cats get spooked. When I lived in New York, there were some times when the cats would suddenly get very twitchy and I'd think, there's something going on, and I could never figure out what it was. I don't know if they're particularly psychic, but they're obviously attuned to something we're not.

One thing I've never understood is showing cats or breeding cats. I came across a cat book a couple of years ago and was horrified to see all of the monster races of cats that are out there. I've always had domestic shorthairs; Abyssinian is the only exotic I've ever had at all. They're still wild animals, despite the fact they're living in the house. What appeals to me is that strange combination of cosy, cuddly, you-can-tickle-their-tummies-and-they'll-lick-your-ear – and there's obviously something about them that's utterly remote from people, and I find that sort of nice.

– A Death in the Family (2017) –

Born in 1975, Caitlin Moran is an English journalist, author and broadcaster and the author of six books, including the runaway bestseller *How to Be a Woman* (2011). 'A Death in the Family' was first published in *The Times*.

I still had the mud on my boots when we took you to the vet, for the last time. I had dug your grave that morning. It didn't take long, in the rain, as you were very small.

You were always just a very small, very silly cat – you were not very clever at all. It was just as well you were beautiful, with your tiny white paws, and perfect tabby stripes, and huge eyes – like foreign moons. That was definitely your strong point. Your beauty.

'That's the stupid cat,' we would say, in the beginning, when visitors came round, and you went purring up to them. 'She's got all the looks – but none of the brains. She's dim as a box of hair. Gorgeous – but simple. It's like living with a beautiful-but-duh Hollywood starlet.'

Because you were so stupid, we didn't know you were ill. We didn't know! You always came and stared at us, intently – like Mog, being confused. You stared at us a lot. That's what Hollywood starlets do! And so we did not know when you stopped staring at us because you were confused – and started staring at us because you were ill, instead. As it turned out, it would have been a long time.

'I'm so sorry. She's got days, at most,' the vet said, when we took you. 'These organs have been failing for a long, long time. But you never can tell, with cats. They hide it.'

In your cage, you blinked at us – shaved; eyes blasted from morphine; a drip in your leg. You sat up very straight – trying, I think, to look dignified.

'Take her home – say goodbye to her,' the vet said, as the girls held her and cried onto her small, confused head. 'Bring her back tomorrow, and we'll . . . let her go.'

We all cried, in the car home – four people, and a tiny parcel of bones and fur. We carried you like you would carry a grail or a crown – you small, silly cat. By then, we knew how important you were.

Because we didn't think you were important, when we got you. Two kittens in a cardboard box, from Battersea – two tabby sisters, with Wedgwood blue eyes. We just thought of you as . . . a delightful treat.

'A cat is a luxurious thing for a house to have,' I thought, as we opened the box, and you and your sister tiptoed out, the size of a purse or glove. 'I will have you here and feed you – and you will lie in front of the fire, and have all the naps I cannot have. You are my lazy decadence proxy. All you have to do, lovely kittens, is be pretty. I ask nothing more of you than I would of a bunch of flowers. Simply – be beautiful. That is your purpose. You are the delightful ornaments of our lives.'

And, of course, you were. You were beautiful, luxurious things.

But a family cat is not just a beautiful thing – as I learnt, over the years. Cats are made of fur because fur absorbs secrets. You can cry into fur. Fur, draped across the heart, will opiate your melancholy. Fur will make you happy again.

Humans need fur, it seems – for all feelings are allowed around fur. Perhaps this is why we buy fur coats – to wear to parties; to feel hot. It's a way of taking our pets, and their kindness, everywhere.

The kindness of pets is the thing. You were very kind, little cat. Sad toddlers would pick you up – often upside down – and be happy again. Angry nine-year-olds would scoop you and take you to their bedroom – to confide their fury. Teenagers – exhausted from GCSEs, or heartbreak, or hospital – would drape you over their faces, or wear you like a stole, and gradually decompress into happy children again.

And the tired parents, at the end of the day, would lie on the sofa with you – you lantern-eyed, unblinking, small, household god – and sigh, 'How has your day been, mate?' and stroke the perfection of your paws.

And I didn't realise what all that meant until I was digging your grave – you watching from the window, like a ghost. To call you 'stupid' was a total misunderstanding of our positions, and the work-ings of the universe. To call you 'stupid' showed how stupid I was. Your entire existence was exquisitely engineered: for a cat is a place where you put all the feelings you can't share with humans.

That's what we have in our houses. Another spe-cies that lives with us, and absorbs our sadness, our loneliness; our anger and excess love – as simpatico as the tiny birds who pick meat from the teeth of crocodiles. They clean our hearts, these tiny cats. We store all our unspoken words in them.

When the vet injected you, and you immediately collapsed – 'She's gone' – I thought how much you had carried around, and yet never once complained.

'You were not stupid,' I said finally, as I put you into the roughly hacked hole at the bottom of the garden. 'You were as clever as love.'

– *from* Jeoffry: The Poet's Cat (2020) –

Oliver Soden is the critically acclaimed author of *Michael Tippett: The Biography* (2019) and *Jeoffry: The Poet's Cat*, a semi-fictionalised biography of poet Christopher Smart's cat, immortalised in Smart's poem, 'Jubilate Agno'. As Soden's book shows, Jeoffry led the rough and tumble life of a London cat long before he went to live with the poet, with a kittenhood spent in a house of ill repute near the Theatre Royal, Drury Lane, and his city wanderings bringing him to the notice of the great and good of eighteenth-century London.

The lustre of Jeoffry's coat was not entirely dimmed by his explorations, but it took an effort of will, from him and from Nancy, to keep it in the condition he liked. Slowly he began to learn the codes of the gang warfare that the cats of Covent Garden waged among the filthy streets; slowly he found his place in the feline hierarchies of the alleyways, knew the bins in which he could scrabble, found which areas were to be avoided and which to be conquered. Awful was the day when Nancy, in a vague effort to keep him from bringing her what was left of the night's pickings, and to stop him from carrying in birds that were only half-dead and would quickly revive in the warmth of her room, spattering the curtains in their fear and knocking into the windows, tied round his neck a pink ribbon threaded through a little bell that she had pulled from one of her more ornamental outfits. It took Jeoffry three days, during which he stayed indoors, sulking, to scratch and tug his way through the ghastly adornment. Only then did he dare to go back outdoors, dignity restored. Not long afterwards, an observer would have noticed his kittenish high jinks changing perceptibly into a seemingly focused stalking of various trails of scent, to which he added the occasional acrid spray of his own.

Not all the cats he came across in the streets of Covent Garden were male, and to the hind quarters of those who allowed him to approach unmolested he paid especial olfactory attention. But let us leave him temporarily in whichever ill-lit and sooty alleyway he has chosen to fight without mercy for his mating rights, in unconscious echo of the transactional activities that were going on in the rooms above his head. Biographers are often accused of being obsessed with their subjects' sex lives; let us say merely that, given the improbability of Jeoffry's ever having been neutered, it is likely that he roamed ever more far and wide in his consuming wanderlust, and over the years unknowingly speckled the city with wriggling broods of ginger and tortoiseshell.

His wanderings eventually took him to the end of Bow Street, and he padded his way along the taverns and coffee houses of Russell Street, and dared the frightening reek of Drury Lane and its film of coal dust on the air. Certain publicans began to mark the hours by his appearances, and grew quite worried on those days when he had been accidentally locked in Nancy's room and did not appear. The demeanour of the tough alley cat soon ceded to an expansive purr if a saucer of milk or plate of scraps seemed likely to appear from any locals who stooped to pet him.

He found a quiet corner on the join between Catherine and Russell Streets where he would usually settle undisturbed each afternoon. Jeoffry came to know one green-gloved hand quite well as it stooped to pet him on its regular arrival from its carriage, haloed by a frothing white cuff, and hovering above a thickly stockinged leg. The owner of the gloved hand had a voice that was rich and resonant, and although Jeoffry understood almost nothing of what was said to him, he felt the low timbre of the voice resonate pleasurably at the fingertips and along his whiskers. The nuzzle from the hand each afternoon became one of Jeoffry's routines, and he was really rather irritated on the days when a higher, whinier voice seemed, in calling away the glove – 'Mr. Garrick, sir, we really must be moving along!' – to curtail their already brief communion. On the glove's disappearance, Jeoffry would settle and each afternoon appraise with his beady unblinking stare

the crowds of people he did not know to be the-
atregoers, arriving in their sedan chairs and carriages, and swarming into a side street to attend
performances at the Theatre Royal, Drury Lane, in
clouds of ruffles and frills, hoops and swords, high
wigs and lemony powder. He watched the coachmen
mill around and spit onto the road, the bearers of
the sedan chairs stretch their limbs and wipe their
brows and scuffle among themselves like any cat.
His ears would reach their way towards the distant
muffle of laughter and applause, the bang of back-
stage scenery and yells of stage crew.

It was common for audiences to make a single
evening's entertainment by taking in an act from an
opera here, an act from a play there, moving from
theatre to opera house and back again before going
on to an afterpiece at the Lincoln's Inn Fields. Jeoffry would watch the crowds moving back and forth
until he knew it was time to leave his own ringside
seat and return to Mother Douglas's house for a few
snatched moments with Nancy before the next of
the night's clients returned. He was a fickle creature,
and on other excursions he began to set up camp by
the stage door of the Theatre Royal in Covent Garden, unaware of or unbothered by the severe rivalry
between the two playhouses. Doorkeepers in both
began to boast of how well-trained was their theatre's cat, which they took to be a good-luck charm
for sales. Jeoffry was happy to wander over to be

scratched or petted, listening with half an ear to the swaddled trumpeting of orchestra or choir.

The fingers of the doorkeeper at the Covent Garden theatre were ridged and swollen, marbled with a rough brown growth that scratched pleasantly at Jeoffry's ears. 'The takings for your oratorio this evening were quite splendid, Mr. Handel,' he would say, as Jeoffry saw a pair of swollen legs make their unsteady way up the two steps and into the waiting carriage. 'We do believe that this kitten here has had a wonderful effect on the attendance. We've named him Samson, in your honour!' Jeoffry ducked beneath a cane, had a vague impression of two milky eyes swivelled in his direction, vague and unseeing beneath a large and trembling wig, and scampered off across the piazza.

Most of his excursions were spent skimming through a world of buckles and ankles, but it took only a scrabble up a tree, his claws sharpening nicely on the rough wood of the bark, or a scramble across a roof, rusted tiles loosening beneath his weight, for his domain to widen, his purview stretch. Scudding clouds of white and grey wigs floated beneath him, and a flow of tri-cornered hats and the canvas tops of carriages pulsed through the tangled arteries of the London streets. But cats are near-sighted. Beyond the realm of his vision was London's usual uproar, red roofs floating beneath a crowd of flags and weather vanes spinning in the smog, the stalagmites of spire, the tangle of masts along the great brown ribbon of the Thames, which froze to a shiny bronze in winter. Looming far above all was the great dome of St. Paul's, its baritone boom ringing out beneath the silvery chiming that assaulted a certain pair of ginger ears, hour upon hour, from a choir of singing saints, St. Peter Upon Cornhill, St. Mary Le Bow, St. Anne, St. Giles in Cripplegate, St. Margaret Lothbury, and the tenor of St. Sepulchre near the Old Bailey, whose bell-ringer would strike an execution knell for the prisoners in nearby Newgate while their last hours seeped away in wide-eyed candle-lit torment, and their last minutes were paraded in front of a baying crowd, which cheered at the clatter of the stool, at the creaking of the rope, at the swinging pair of dusty shoes, just brushing an inquisitive ginger nose as, on one of Jeoffry's walks through the city, he stumbled upon the reek of death.

It was the November of 1755, by which time Jeoffry, as old as the decade, had grown adept at the navigation of the London streets. He was settled once again in his regular spot opposite the Drury Lane Theatre. For nearly an hour he had been watching a steady and mysterious stream of people go inside. A babel of unknown languages shot its way across the street and into his ears, and his claws flexed with longing as he saw, being carried into the theatre, lustrous reels of brightly coloured silks, handfuls of beads, headdresses and swords and, at one astonishing moment, as the light began to dim on that cold wintry afternoon, a procession of lustrous yellow globes bobbing their way into the building, held aloft on sticks, as if the stars of the sky had fallen to earth and were floating along the chilly street. They were Chinese lanterns, lit from within by candles – but little did Jeoffry know that the theatre was hosting a spectacular ballet called Les Fêtes Chinoises. When a dragon arrived, its garishly painted visage all but hiding the men who were carrying it along the road and into the theatre, he considered turning tail and fleeing, but held his ground. Thirty minutes later the cold threatened to become intolerable, and Jeoffry was just about to return home, when a carriage drew up that he knew, somehow, as cats can know things they should not, was different from the other vehicles that thundered their way in and out of his life. Crowds were gathered, shouting, cheering. The coachmen seemed dressed with especial extravagance. A trumpeter heralded the opening of the door; a river of green (or so Jeoffry perceived it) suddenly splashed from the door of the carriage, which opened (Jeoffry prowled closer) to reveal a grand boot, a buckle of astonishing glitter, a white-stockinged leg into which a garter of gold thread appeared to slice painfully. Jeoffry had slunk close enough now to put a tentative paw out onto the green river, to look up into a blue waistcoat of impossible luxury, and beyond it, rolls of neck. The face, all but hidden by the brocaded stomach beneath it, peered mistily down, and look at Jeoffry. Jeoffry looked up into the face. The face went on its way, but had smiled, briefly. For a cat may look at a king.

CHRISTINA ROSSETTI

– On the Death of a Cat, a Friend of Mine, Aged Ten Years and a Half –

Christina Georgina Rossetti (1830–1894) was an English poet most famous for her romantic, devotional and children's poems, including *Goblin Market and Other Poems* (1862), which established her as the most accomplished female poet of the late nineteenth century. She also wrote the words of two Christmas carols, 'In the Bleak Midwinter' and 'Love Came Down at Christmas'. She was a sister of the artist and poet Dante Gabriel Rossetti and features in several of his paintings.

Who shall tell the lady's grief
  When her Cat was past relief?
Who shall number the hot tears
Shed o'er her, beloved for years?
Who shall say the dark dismay
Which her dying caused that day?

Come, ye Muses, one and all,
Come obedient to my call.
Come and mourn, with tuneful breath,
Each one for a separate death;
And while you in numbers sigh,
I will sing her elegy.

Of a noble race she came,
And Grimalkin was her name.
Young and old full many a mouse
Felt the prowess of her house:
Weak and strong full many a rat
Cowered beneath her crushing pat:
And the birds around the place
Shrank from her too close embrace.
But one night, reft of her strength,
She laid down and died at length:
Lay a kitten by her side,
In whose life the mother died.
Spare her line and lineage,
Guard her kitten's tender age,
And that kitten's name as wide
Shall be known as her's that died.

And whoever passes by
The poor grave where Puss doth lie,
Softly, softly let him tread,
Nor disturb her narrow bed.

MARY GAITSKILL

– *from* Lost Cat (2020) –

Mary Gaitskill is a critically acclaimed novelist, short-story writer and essayist. She was born in Kentucky, sold flowers in San Francisco as a teenage runaway and now lives in Brooklyn. In 2002 she was awarded a Guggenheim Fellowship, and that same year her story 'Secretary', from the collection *Bad Behaviour*, was made into a film.

Last year I lost my cat Gattino. He was very young, at seven months barely an adolescent. He is probably dead but I don't know for certain. For two weeks after he disappeared people claimed to have seen him; I trusted two of the claims because Gattino was blind in one eye, and both people told me that when they'd caught him in their headlights, only one eye shone back. One guy, who said he saw my cat trying to scavenge from a garbage can, said that he'd 'looked really thin, like the runt of the litter'. The pathetic words struck my heart. But I heard something besides the words, something in the coarse, vibrant tone of the man's voice that immediately made another emotional picture of the cat: back arched, face afraid but excited, brimming and ready before he jumped and ran, tail defiant, tensile and crooked. Afraid but ready; startled by a large male, that's how he would've been. Even if he was weak with hunger. He had guts, this cat.

Gattino disappeared two and a half months after we moved. Our new house is on the outskirts of a college campus near a wildlife preserve. There are wooded areas in all directions, and many homes with decrepit outbuildings sit heavily, darkly low behind trees, in thick foliage. I spent hours at a time wandering around calling Gattino. I put food out. I put a trap out. I put hundreds of flyers up, I walked around knocking on doors, asking people if I could look in their shed or under their porch. I contacted all the vets in the area. Every few days, someone would call and say they had seen a cat in a parking lot or behind their dorm. I would go and sometimes glimpse a grizzled adult melting away into the woods, or behind a building or under a parked car.

After two weeks there were no more sightings. I caught three feral cats in my trap and let them go. It began to snow. Still searching, I would sometimes see little cat tracks in the snow; near dumpsters full of garbage, I also saw prints made by bobcats or coyotes. When the temperature went below freezing, there was icy rain. I kept looking. A year later I still had not stopped.

Six months after Gattino disappeared my husband and I were sitting in a restaurant having dinner with some people he had recently met, including an intellectual writer we both admired. The writer had considered buying the house we were living in and he wanted to know how we liked it. I said it was nice but it had been partly spoiled for me by the loss of our cat. I told him the story and he said, 'Oh, that was your trauma, was it?'

I said yes. Yes, it was a trauma.

You could say he was unkind. You could say I was silly. You could say he was priggish. You could say I was weak.

A few weeks earlier, I had an email exchange with my sister Martha on the subject of trauma, or rather tragedy. Our other sister, Jane, had just decided not to euthanize her dying cat because she thought her little girls could not bear it; she didn't think she could bear it. Jane lives in chronic pain so great that sometimes she cannot move normally. She is under great financial stress and is often responsible for the care of her mother-in-law as well as the orphaned children of her sister-in-law who died of cancer. But it was her cat's approaching death that made her cry so that her children were frightened. 'This is awful,' said Martha. 'It is not helping that cat to keep him alive, it's just prolonging his suffering. It's selfish.'

Martha is in a lot of pain too, most of it related to diabetes and fibromyalgia. Her feet hurt so badly she can't walk longer than five minutes. She just lost her job and is applying for disability which, because it's become almost impossible to get, she may not get, and which, if she does get, will not be enough to live on, and we will have to help her. We already have to help her because her COBRA payments are so high that her unemployment isn't enough to cover them. This is painful for her too; she doesn't want to be the one everybody has to help. And so she tries to help us. She has had cats for years, and so knows a lot about them; she wanted to help Jane by giving her advice, and she sent me several emails wondering about the best way to do it. Finally she forwarded me the message she had sent to Jane, in which she urged her to put the cat down. When she didn't hear from Jane, she emailed me some more, agonizing over whether or not Jane was angry at her, and wondering what decision Jane would make regarding the cat. She said, 'I'm afraid this is going to turn into an avoidable tragedy.'

Impatient by then, I told her that she should trust Jane to make the right decision. I said, this is sad, not tragic. Tragedy is thousands of people dying slowly of war and disease, injury and malnutrition. It's Hurricane Katrina, it's the war in Iraq, it's the earthquake in China. It's not one creature dying of old age.

After I sent the email, I looked up the word 'tragic'. According to *Webster's College Dictionary*, I was wrong; their second definition of the word is 'extremely mournful, melancholy or pathetic'. I emailed Martha and admitted I'd been wrong, at least technically. I added that I still thought she was being hysterical. She didn't answer me. Maybe she was right not to.

I found Gattino in Italy. I was in Tuscany at a place called Santa Maddalena run by a woman named Beatrice von Rezzori who, in honor of her deceased husband, a writer, has made her estate into a small retreat for writers. When Beatrice learned that I love cats, she told me that down the road from her two old women were feeding a yard full of semi-wild cats, including a litter of kittens who were very sick and going blind. Maybe, she said, I could help them out. No, I said, I wasn't in Italy to do that, and anyway, having done it before, I know it isn't an easy thing to trap and tame a feral kitten.

The next week one of her assistants, who was driving me into the village, asked if I wanted to see some kittens. Sure, I said, not making the connection. We stopped by an old farmhouse. A gnarled woman sitting in a wheelchair covered with towels and a thin blanket greeted the assistant without looking at me. Scrawny cats with long legs and narrow ferret hips stalked or lay about in the buggy, overgrown yard. Two kittens, their eyes gummed up with yellow fluid and flies swarming around their asses, were obviously sick but still lively – when I bent to touch them, they ran away. But a third kitten, smaller and bonier than the other two, tottered up to me mewing weakly, his eyes almost glued shut. He was a tabby, soft gray with strong black stripes. He had a long jaw and a big nose shaped like an eraser you'd stick on the end of a pencil. His big-nosed head was goblin-ish on his emaciated pot-bellied body, his long legs almost grotesque. His asshole seemed disproportionately big on his starved rear. Dazedly, he let me stroke his bony back – tentatively, he lifted his pitiful tail. I asked the assistant if she would help me take the kittens to a veterinarian and she agreed; this had no doubt been the idea all along.

The healthier kittens scampered away as we approached and hid in a collapsing barn; we were only able to collect the tabby. When we put him in the carrier, he forced open his eyes with a mighty effort, took a good look at us, hissed, tried to arch his back and fell over. But he let the vets handle him. When they tipped him forward and lifted his tail to check his sex, he had a delicate, nearly human look of puzzled dignity in his one half-good eye, while his blunt muzzle expressed stoic animality. It was a comical and touching face.

They kept him for three days. When I came to pick him up, they told me he would need weeks of care, involving eye ointment, ear drops and nose drops. The Baroness suggested I bring him home to America. No, I said, not possible. My husband was coming to meet me in a month and we were going to travel for two weeks; we couldn't take him with us. I would care for him and by the time I left, he should be well enough to go back to the yard with a fighting chance.

So I called him 'Chance'. I liked Chance as I like all kittens; he liked me as a food dispenser. He looked at me neutrally, as if I were one more creature in the world, albeit a useful one. I had to worm him, de-flea him and wash encrusted shit off his tail. He squirmed when I put the medicine in his eyes and ears, but he never tried to scratch me – I think because he wasn't absolutely certain of how I might react if he did. He tolerated my petting him, but seemed to find it a novel sensation rather than a pleasure.

Then one day he looked at me differently. I don't know exactly when it happened – I may not have noticed the first time. But he began to raise his head when I came into the room, to look at me intently. I can't say for certain what the look meant; I don't know how animals think or feel. But it seemed that he was looking at me with love. He followed me around my apartment. He sat in my lap when I worked at my desk. He came into my bed and slept with me; he lulled himself to sleep by gnawing softly on my fingers. When I petted him, his body would rise into my hand. If my face were close to him, he would reach out with his paw and stroke my cheek.

Sometimes, I would walk on the dusty roads surrounding Santa Maddalena and think about my father, talking to him in my mind. My father had landed in Italy during the Second World War; he was part of the Anzio invasion. After the war he returned as a visitor with my mother, to Naples and to Rome. There is a picture of him standing against an ancient wall wearing a suit and a beret; he looks elegant, formidable and at the same time tentative, nearly shy. On my walks I carried a large, beautiful marble that had belonged to my father; sometimes I took it out of my pocket and held it up in the sun as if it might function as a conduit for his soul. My father died a slow painful death of cancer, refusing treatment of any kind for as long as he was able to make himself understood, gasping, 'No doctors, no doctors.' My mother had left him years before; my sisters and I tended to him, but inadequately, and too late – he had been sick for months, unable to eat for at least weeks before we became aware of his condition. During those weeks I thought of calling him; if I had I would've known immediately that he was dying. But I didn't call. He was difficult, and none of us called him often.

My husband did not like the name Chance and I wasn't sure I did either; he suggested McFate, and so I tried it out. McFate grew stronger, grew a certain one-eyed rakishness, an engaged forward quality to his ears and the attitude of his neck that was gallant in his fragile body. He put on weight, and his long legs and tail became *soigné*, not grotesque. He had strong necklace markings on his throat; when he rolled on his back for me to pet him, his belly was beige and spotted like an ocelot. In a confident mood, he was like a little gangster in a zoot suit. Pensive, he was still delicate; his heart seemed closer to the surface than normal, and when I held him against me, it beat very fast and light. McFate was too big and heartless a name for such a small fleet-hearted creature. '*Mio Gattino,*' I whispered, in a language I don't speak to a creature who didn't understand words. '*Mio dolce piccolo gatto.*'

One night when he was lying on his back in my lap, purring, I saw something flash across the floor; it was a small, sky-blue marble rolling out from under the dresser and across the floor. It stopped in the middle of the floor. It was beautiful, bright, and something not visible to me had set it in motion. It seemed a magical and forgiving omen, like the presence of this loving little cat. I put it on the windowsill next to my father's marble.

I spoke to my husband about taking Gattino home with us. I said I had fallen in love with the cat, and that I was afraid that by exposing him to human love I had awakened in him a need that was unnatural, that if I left him he would suffer from the lack of human attention that he never would have known had I not appeared in his yard. My husband said,

'Oh no, Mary . . .' but in a bemused tone.

I would understand if he'd said it in a harsher tone. Many people would consider my feelings neurotic, a projection onto an animal of my own need. Many people would consider it almost offensive for me to lavish such love on an animal when I have by some standards failed to love my fellow beings: for example, orphaned children who suffer every day, not one of whom I have adopted. But I have loved people; I have loved children. And it seems that what happened between me and the children I chose to love was a version of what I was afraid would happen to the kitten. Human love is grossly flawed, and even when it isn't, people routinely misunderstand it, reject it, use it or manipulate it. It is hard to protect a person you love from pain because people often choose pain; *I* am a person who often chooses pain. An animal will never choose pain; an animal can receive love far more easily than even a very young human. And so I thought it should be possible to shelter a kitten with love.

I made arrangements with the vet to get me a cat passport; Gattino endured the injection of an identifying microchip into his slim shoulder. Beatrice said she could not keep him in her house, and so I made arrangements for the vet to board him for the two weeks Peter and I traveled.

Peter arrived; Gattino looked at him and hid under the dresser. Peter crouched down and talked to him softly. Then he and I lay on the bed and held each other. In a flash, Gattino grasped the situation: the male had come. He was friendly. We could all be together now. He came onto the bed, sat on Peter's chest and purred thunderously. He stayed on Peter's chest all night.

We took him to the veterinarian the next day. Their kennel was not the quiet, cat-only quarters one finds at upscale American animal hospitals. It was a common area that smelled of disinfectant and fear. The vet put Gattino in a cage near that of a huge enraged dog that barked and growled, lunging against the door of its kennel. Gattino looked at me and began to cry. I cried too. The dog raged. There was a little bed in Gattino's cage and he hid behind it, then defiantly lifted his head to face the gigantic growling; that is when I first saw that terrified but ready expression, that willingness to meet whatever was coming, regardless of its size or its ferocity.

When we left the vet I was crying absurdly hard. But I was not crying exclusively about the kitten, any more than my sister Jane was crying exclusively about euthanizing her old cat. At the time I didn't realize it, but I was, among other things, crying about the children I once thought of as mine.

– *from* My Life So Far, By Pard (2016) –

Ursula K. Le Guin (1929–2018) was an American author of speculative fiction, realistic fiction, non-fiction, screenplays, librettos, essays, poetry, speeches, translations, literary critiques and children's fiction. She was primarily known for her novels set in the fictional world of Earthsea, but was also the author of a number of 'chapbooks', including *My Life So Far, by Pard*, which has been described as 'a thoughtful, truthful autobiography, translated from the Feline by Ursula K. Le Guin.' In his autobiography, Pard relates how he first met the other inhabitants of his forever home, and navigated his way through the strangenesses of the world around him.

There was so much strangeness in the strange place that when I met the old queen and the younger aunty humans they were just parts of it. But they distinctly had good intentions, and good manners, too, admiring me, holding out their knuckles to me like noses, and making no effort to hug. So I purred loudly and kept my tail so straight up that the end of it fell over onto my back, which pleased them, and there was mutual pleasantness. And so I left there and came here with them.

I cried very loudly in the roaring moving roomthing on the way here, because I thought the awfulness and strangeness was all happening over again forever. I still always think that when they put me in the box that smells of fear and the roaring moving room-thing. But except for that I have hardly cried at all since coming here.

The aunty human went away and left me with the old queen and an old tom. I was distrustful of him at first, but my fears were groundless. When he sits down he has an excellent thing, a lap. Other humans have them, but his is mine. It is full of quietness and fondness. The old queen sometimes pats hers and says *prrt?* and I know perfectly well what she means; but I only use one lap, his. What I like to use about her is the place behind her knees on the bed, and the top of her head, which having a kind of fur reminds me a little of my Mother, so sometimes I get on the pillow with it and knead it. This works best when she is asleep.

The kibbles here are of different species and varying quality. They are let loose from their boxes and bags into my bowl twice a day at the appointed time. Most of them are good, but the small dark kind taste rather nasty and I don't hunt them down till I really need them. Recently a large new breed appeared that taste excellent, almost as good as greenies.

No other kibble is as good as a greeny. And greenies often fly – the old tom and queen see to it that they do – and I chase them across the floor, and pursue them under things, and knock them right out of the air. Hunting is very exciting and satisfactory, especially when the prey moves. When I first came here I was barely out of kittenhood and constantly in search of excitement. Here and there, though never in my bowl, I found what I thought was a lively kind of kibble, running around, hiding under things, even flying sometimes. I hunted them for quite a while and caught a great many, but they never did taste very good. I gave up hunting them at last, admitting that beetles are an inferior form of kibble. Still, it was fun to hunt them.

It is not fun to hunt mice. It is exciting in an intense, terrible way. If there is a mouse, I cannot think of anything else. I cannot sleep. I cannot eat kibbles. I can only smell and hear and think of mouse. I don't understand this, and it makes me unhappy. But when the mouse comes out of hiding I have to hunt it and catch it. I always catch it. And then what? It isn't a kibble, it isn't to eat. It's much bigger, and furry, who wants to eat a huge fur-coated kibble? It is a wonderful toy while it plays, but after a while it begins to run down and stops moving. So I bring it to the old queen, who is good with toys and makes them move. But if it is a mouse, she leaps up and does shouting and hurls the mouse off the bed, and there is great unpleasantness.

All the same, much as I dislike unpleasantness, I cannot leave the mouse. Usually it begins moving again, and sometimes even gets away and escapes into the outside, but not often. When it runs down altogether it is taken away. Then I can sleep and be happy.

The outside is somewhat like mice: it is too exciting. It makes anxiety. I want to go there and then when I am there I want to come inside again. I am used to walls. Walls are good, they limit things. There is no limit to the outside. It is crowded with endless things and beings, pathways and pathless-nesses, movements, sounds, tiny noises in the earth and behind every leaf, huge bangs and clamor from where the roaring things rush by and the terrible dogs pull their humans along by straps and nothing makes sense. But then, it is all exciting. There are the green leaves to eat, and then come in and throw them up on the rug. There are the beings that fly, not only little ones like beetles but ones the size of mice and even bigger. When I see them I say some-thing to them I never say to anybody else, a kind of little clicking. I know they are to hunt. How could I catch a flying kibble bigger than a mouse, and what would I do with it if I caught it? But still when I see one, even through the window, I crouch to spring and whisper k-k-k-k-k-k-k to lure it closer.

It is very puzzling, the outside, and very danger-ous. I know that, and mostly I stay in sight of the old queen or tom, and always I know the quickest path straight back to the door, my door, into my walls, into my place.

But there are the smells outside, the endless, rich, piercing, mysterious smells, and I want to go back out, and smell each leaf and stick and track for a long time, and walk on the strange paths of dirt and grass, in the danger.

Yet while I am there I want to be back inside with the old slow tom and queen, where things happen slowly and when they should happen and the kibbles are in the bowl morning and evening, where I can lie in the sun and look through the window at the outside without being in its danger, or curl up on the tom's lap or the queen's head and hear the purring and be happy.

There is so much mystery always that adding all the outside to it is too much for me.

Inside, I am troubled only when the old tom and queen go away for a long time, which they don't do often any more, but when they do some of the strangeness gets into the house, the kibbles become irregular, and I am not at peace.

And my peace is disturbed when the young queens come to make the noise machine go on the floors. The anxiety of the horrible roaring noise drives me to do foolish things like trying to hide behind the thing the old queen always sits in front of staring at instead of paying attention to me. I am not supposed to go behind it, and unpleasantness occurs when I insist on doing so. Perhaps the unpleasantness of the noise machines drives me to make more unpleasantness. I don't know. Sometimes I decide to go behind the thing simply because as I lie on the desk beside her in peaceful companionship, I get bored with her staring at it and ignoring me, and know I can change that by going where I am not to go.

Recently when I did that and wouldn't stop doing it we both got so upset that the old queen did shouting, swatted me, and pulled my tail, and I actually glared and cursed her.

Soon after, she apologised and made amends. I did not. Cats have no amends to make. But we were both relieved that the unpleasantness was ended.

Since then, when I start to go around behind the thing she stares at, instead of attempting to exert domination and causing anxiety to us both she begins to scratch my jowls and chin most irresistibly. So I stop where I am and do not resist the irresistibility, and as she finds this irresistible too, there is pleasantness and good feeling. I just started around behind a minute ago, but settled down for a thorough jowl-rub on both sides while warmth and good feelings were exchanged.

REBECCA WEST

– *from* Why My Mother was Frightened of Cats (1956) –

Rebecca West (1892–1983) (whose real name was Cicily Isabel Fairfield) was a British author, journalist, literary critic and travel writer whose major works include *Black Lamb and Grey Falcon* (1941), *A Train of Powder* (1955), her coverage of the Nuremberg trials, and *The New Meaning of Treason* (1964), a study of the trial of the British fascist William Joyce, 'Lord Haw-Haw'. Despite being abandoned by her father at the age of eight and later enduring various struggles as an unmarried mother, her essays on family life resonate with affection and wit.

For me to keep a cat has all the excitement of a forbidden love-affair, for my mother belonged to that unhappy race which feels a mysterious fear of cats. If she found herself in a room with the most innocent and ravishing of cats, she would start to her feet and wring her hands, the long supple hands of a pianist, and she would cry, 'Take it away! Take it away!' while she shut her eyes so that she need not see the loathsome object. I never reproached my mother even in my own mind for these paroxysms, for I was a soldier's daughter, and it was well-known that the most venerable general of that day, Lord Roberts, suffered from the same malady. He would turn and run if a cat walked towards him on the parade-ground; and I quite realised that if Lord Roberts could not control this terror my mother could not be expected to do better. So there was no ill-feeling between us. Yet not to have a cat inflicted a great hardship on me.[. . .] I was like a woman who had wanted children all her life and at last finds herself free to become a mother and then feels panic. I thought I would never be able to rear a cat, I felt sure I would give it the wrong food, I saw a stern vet reproaching me by my cat's basket and asking me if I had not let my professional duties come between my duty to my cat. But my son had a cat, and when he went on a holiday he called on me and dropped the cat into the drawing-room window, saying, 'Look after Poughkeepsie till I come back.'

Poughkeepsie is the name of an American town, a delightful name in English wars, for it is an Indian name and evokes the charm of Fenimore Cooper and the United States when they were innocent and idyllic. [. . .] She enchanted us, and settled all my misgivings. [. . .]

This was, of course, not a serious relationship, not a true sample of the joys and sorrows which cats can bring us. It was the equivalent of the love-affair with a chorus-girl which is not so much love as an introduction to the technique of love. But I did not understand that, and when my son offered me one of Poughkeepsie's kittens I accepted it in the belief that it would give the same sort of pleasure as its mother. But the first sight of the kitten dispelled this idea. He was physically frivolous, a ball of orange fluff with topaz eyes, he might have been the sort of Christmas present the more expensive stores in New York think up, and have a bottle of scent inside him; yet he was a serious-minded cat. When he looked at one, he referred what he saw to a store of innate knowledge and a firm tradition, and passed a judgement on one which he at once prudently put by for later use. There was also a sense of frustration about him which seemed to spring from his inability to take part in the conversation.

Without doubt, cats are intellectuals who have been, by some mysterious decree of Providence, deprived of the comfort of the word. He at once, by a single action, declared his character and moulded it. We had bought a new house, but could not get into it, and in the meantime had taken a house of a more seigniorial sort than we ordinarily inhabited. Our gardens were superb. Poughkeepsie had had social ambitions but not a rag of pedigree; and the father of this new kitten had been a farm labourer, who earned a meagre living by keeping down the rats in a granary. The kitten's name was plain Pounce, as it might have been Untel. But the grandeur of the surroundings was entirely to his taste. He did not merely accept them, he savoured them, he turned them over on his tongue. Out he went across the lawn with the two cedars, down the stone steps to the terrace with its high banks of lupins, his tail straight up and swaying with satisfaction. Along the yew walk he went to the rose-garden, not hurrying it, taking it at a processional pace, past the carousel of lily-beds to the lake of nenuphars. There he went too far. The tiny creature leaped to the furthest conceivable extreme of ambition. He tried to walk on the water. Before we could get to him he was a snuffling and scrambling rag of wet fur. Somebody had laughed. His pride was cut to the quick. [...] How should a kitten grasp the idea of 'making a fool of oneself,' with all its implications, which involve self-respect, the importance we attach to the opinion of others, and our tendency to laugh when someone has a physical misadventure?

But all this Pounce realised, and more besides. [. . .] In later years he used to kiss my hand when I stroked him. But always before the kiss he gave me a hard stare. 'If I give her an inch, will she take an ell? Will she trespass on the secret places of my being if I let her be too familiar?' He took the risk, but he was always sensible that it was a risk. This reserve and withdrawal were the more fascinating because he was a superb comedian, specialising in a sort of gymnastic satire.

The house where we were living was not as good as its gardens, for its owner had allowed an interior decorator to transform its seventeenth-century rooms into the stage set of a provincial production of Cyrano de Bergerac or The Three Musketeers. The place was cluttered with refectory tables and high-backed chairs which evoked bad actors sweeping off huge hats adorned with moulting feathers and declaiming alexandrines at bad actresses sweeping blowsy curtseys. These were depressing surroundings, particularly when the summer ended and war broke out, and we were unable to move away. But they were lightened by the athletic ridicule with which Pounce treated this furniture which was worse than Porte St. Martin stuff, because it was obviously very expensive. [. . .]

The owner of the house never knew what Pounce had thought of her treasures. It is easy to say that Pounce had formed no critical judgement of the furniture, and that we ascribed wit to him only because he was lithe and quick as we imagine wit would be if it had a corporeal shape. It was not easy to maintain that scepticism if one lived with Pounce. At least one had to admit that a comic genius was presiding over Pounce's destiny. There was, for example, the mistake made by the vet. Nocturnal scufflings in the night, and a horrid rent in one of Pounce's exquisitely shaped ears, made me realise that I must have him doctored. I would gladly have left him the pleasures of love, but on the other hand it was cruel to ask Voltaire to live the life of Casanova. He went to the vet and stayed with him for two days. When he returned we noted two things: a new lustre on his fur which we had not remarked before, and a strange contentment, not quite of the sort we would have expected as the result of his new state. This was not resignation. Rather did it remind me of the active gloating which I had noted in a famous lawyer when I sat with him in his garden the day after he had vanquished his only serious rival at the bar. We had another surprise during the night, when there were again scufflings in the shrubbery, again love cries. But one of the gardeners had a tom-cat. All the same, Pounce was out and did not come back till morning.

Then a note came from the vet. There had been a mistake that for him was terrible. At the same time that we had left Pounce at the surgery, the vet had received a superb young tom-cat, the offspring of a champion sire and dam, himself destined to be a champion sire, in order that he should be put in perfect condition for his first show. By some extraordinary accident the pedigree tom had been castrated and the plebeian Pounce had been groomed for appearance at a show which would never have let him inside its doors. Obviously this accident was the result of carelessness on the part of the vet's assistants. Pounce cannot really have said to the pedigree tom: 'Look here, old man, I can let you in on a good thing. They're going to do an operation on me which doesn't hurt, and it means I'll be on velvet for the rest of my life. Now, I like you, I can see you're a thoroughly good chap, and I'll let you have the operation instead of me, if you like. It will mean I will have to wait my turn, but I don't care, I'm the sort of man who enjoys doing a friend a favour.' Yet, as we took him to the vet for the second time, there was a gloomy composure and defiant humour in his limpid stare. He might have been saying, 'Well, I couldn't expect to get away with it forever. But at any rate, you weren't able to do me out of that last night in the shrubbery.'

Never did Pounce simply live. He always made a comment on life as he lived it. [. . .]

He lay at my husband's feet during breakfast, and would go with him to the front door when it was time for him to go to his work. Then came the comment. The door once closed, he would slowly turn round and cross the hall to the sofa, and curl up on its cushions with a sad little shake of the head. 'There is nothing to do but sleep till he comes back.' I was wounded a little when he decided not to make me the object of his adoration. I was content to love rather than be loved, and he was really very kind and companionable. [. . .]

I used to wonder why my mother, who was right about almost everything, should have been so wrong about cats. Then suddenly a disquieting fact was brought to my notice. We lived on the top floor of the apartment house, and outside our windows a cornice ran round the four sides of the building.

This Pounce used as a playground, to take the air and exercise his sense of power by ordering the pigeons he found there to take off into the empyrean, and we used to watch him complacently. But it now appeared that he had been using the cornice for other and odious purposes. He had been visiting a neighbour of ours. Not all our neighbours, only one. He had walked past the window of hosts who would have been glad to entertain him, who cried 'Pussy, pussy' as he went by, imagining him to be innocent and playful like themselves, and he went round two sides of the building to the apartment furthest from ours, to call on Mr. Gubbins: the one person among our neighbours who belonged to the same unhappy race as my mother, who feared cats. The abominable genius of Pounce not only led him to this victim but indicated to him the moments when he was alone and most vulnerable. The poor man suffered from the fear of cats in an even more intense form than my mother. When he saw a cat he became paralysed. Pounce used to visit him when he was having a bath. [. . .] When Pounce dropped into his bathroom and sat down on his haunches and looked at Mr. Gubbins, the poor man's deplorable and pendulous nakedness was then congealed. The poor man could not get to his bath-towel, to his bell, to his door; he could only utter loud wordless groans for help. [. . .]

[. . .] He would have never known how to find his tormentor if he had not seen a photograph of me and my cat outside a photographer's office. When I received the letter from Mr. Gubbins which told me of this shocking sadistic crime, the criminal was sitting at my feet. Never had he looked more beautiful. The subtle lines of his muscle gave him a strong resemblance to Sarah Bernhardt in her youth; his fur, orange and gold and flame and snow- white, had the brilliance and lustre and depth which is given by health and youth; and his purr had the tone of a cello.

I gasped. Lovely, and so odious! [. . .] I knew then that my mother had had some cause for her fear of cats. Mercifully, I was soon able to remove Pounce out of the way of temptation, for our own house in the country became available. Once we were installed there he again became innocent.

[. . .] He was always very kind to us when we were ill, and would come and lie on our beds, though he would do that at no other time. But always in his expressions remained a measure of reserve. He never lost his fear that if he encouraged us we might get too familiar.

When we had been in London and he heard the horn of our automobile, he always recognised it and would rush out into the yard. But as we got out of the automobile he would turn his back on us and walk slowly away, as if he had been there by pure chance. One could not be too careful. [. . .]

[. . .] At last there came a time when we noted

that Pounce's fur was not so brilliant as it had been, that his profile was blunted and no longer recalled the young Sarah Bernhardt, that when he wanted to come in from the garden he mewed for us to open the French window, instead of jumping up to the little high window we always left wide for him. A visitor said, 'That cat is beginning to look his age,' and our hearts contracted. But he had a very happy old age. He was the very pattern of a crusty but contented old bachelor. [. . .]

One autumn morning Madame McVey told me that he had not eaten at all the previous day, and later I looked out of my window at the grassy slope that drops from my house, and I saw under the branch of the great cedar a singular group. Gathered in a circle were Pounce, a large black and white cat which I had never seen before, two hen pheasants, and a cock pheasant. This is not so strange as it might appear. The pheasants in the woods round our house use our garden as a sanctuary, and they were so much larger than Pounce that he had always been on peaceable terms with them, though not so far as I had seen, in such close intimacy as this. Presently the pheasants whirred up into the tree, the black and white cat glided into the long grass, and Pounce came up the slope to the house. As he drew nearer I saw that his fur was harsh and the pride of his body had left him. When I picked him up he felt not quite a whole person, but like bones and muscles and flesh assembled within a pelt. We sent for the vet, who could not come till the next day, and we tried to keep Pounce in the house, for it was cold. But he kept on escaping into the garden and curling up at one particular spot in a flower-bed, where the earth is banked up against the wall of the house; and we had to keep on bringing him back into the warmth. I was in the act of picking him out of the flower-bed when the vet drove up and I called to him, 'This is the fifth time I have done this.' He answered gravely, 'That is a bad sign. They always seek a strange place to lie down, often quite an uncomfortable one, when they are going to die,' and he took Pounce from me and began to feel his body for the lump which he was going to find very easily. When he had spoken the bad news, Pounce jumped out of his arms and walked towards me, staggering a little, but keeping on. We were back where we began. It was again as it had been when he was a kitten and tried to walk on the water among the nenuphars. He had shrunk, he looked quite small; and he had trusted himself to a surface that had looked as if it would bear his weight for ever, and now it was not keeping its promise, it was letting him fall through into a chill engulfing element. But he felt that all would not be lost, that nearly all would be saved, if he retained his dignity, and he tried to bear himself like a tiger. At last I knew why my mother was frightened of cats. It was evidently not the same reason why Lord Roberts and Mr. Gubbins hate them. Cats can be depended upon to find an infinite number of ways of disconcerting human beings. But I did not doubt that my mother, always prophetic about me, had foreseen the state in which I found myself at that moment. But I had understood the warning thirteen years too late. This mattered, however, not at all, for she was wrong. The price I paid was enormous but I got full value for it.

– An Inscription at St. Augustine with St. Faith's Church –

On 9 September 1940, heavy bombing from German forces destroyed a church in the City of London, St. Augustine with St. Faith's Church, on Watling Street, just east of St. Paul's Cathedral. But amid the rubble, a resourceful cat and her kitten survived against the odds. Later named 'Faith', a plaque was erected in the only remaining part of the church, the tower, and her fame spread. So legendary had this brave church cat become, that years later, her death was reported in national newspapers on four continents and she even had her own obituary in *Time* magazine.

'Faith'

O ur dear little church cat of St. Augustine and St. Faith.

The bravest cat in the world.

On Monday, September 9th, 1940, she endured horrors and perils beyond the power of words to tell.

Shielding her kitten in a sort of recess in the house (a spot she selected three days before the tragedy occurred), she sat the whole frightful night of bombing and fire, guarding her little kitten.

The roofs and masonry exploded. The whole house blazed. Four floors fell through in front of her. Fire and water and ruin all round her.

Yet she stayed calm and steadfast and waited for help.

We rescued her in the early morning while the place was still burning, and

By the mercy of Almighty God, she and her kitten were not only saved, but unhurt.

God be praised and thanked for His goodness and mercy to our dear little pet.

BOHUMIL HRABAL

– *from* All My Cats (1965) –

Translated from the Czech by Paul Wilson (2019)

Bohumil Hrabal (1914–1997) was a celebrated Czech
writer. The coincidence of cruelty and beauty is a fre-
quent theme in his writing and in *All My Cats*, his con-
fessional memoir written in the wake of a serious car
accident, the author is overwhelmed both by the brutal
demands of his responsibility for so many cats, and his
love and empathy for them.

When we'd all made it through the winter,
and spring had arrived, a small tabby cat
showed up at our place and she was pregnant. By
this time, Blackie was pregnant, too. The two cats
loved each other and, because they were expecting,
they followed me around incessantly. Wherever I
went, they went, too, and I was always tripping over
them, but nothing upset them as long as they could
be with me. They would gaze at me adoringly and
I knew they were looking to me to help them when
their time came.

My neighbor, Mr. Eliáš, made me a bird feeder,
an absurd looking contraption cobbled together
from an old radio. He'd removed the guts, staved
in the front panel, mounted it on a base that he fas-
tened to a post, then drove the post into the ground

outside his window, right where there was a break in the fence. Whenever I arrived at the cottage to tend to my cats and to write, I'd crumble some dry bread and oatmeal into the feeder for the sparrows and the titmice and the occasional jay.

I was horrified at the prospect of the cats having kittens. I was afraid they'd have them in my bed, as Blackie's mother, Máca, had done. I worried about what we'd do with so many kittens and it killed me to think that if each cat had four kittens, I'd have to drown them. Not all of them, I'd leave the mothers two kittens each, but I'd still have to be the executioner.

At the time, my wife would spend most of the day cooking for the cats and doling out milk for them, but the main problem was they were happiest in the kitchen and the room reeked of cats. I was so used to them I couldn't smell it myself, but anyone who came to visit would always sniff the air. The cats would do their business, not just in the basin filled with sand, but sometimes in the corner of the kitchen, or the pantry, and when they had diarrhea, they'd poo wherever it caught up with them, and my wife would go around in a permanent state of seething reproach. She was sick and tired of washing the sheets and cleaning up the mess on the carpet, so I would do it. Every weekend I'd wipe up after the cats, first with a paper towel and then with a damp rag, and sometimes my nerves would snap and I'd shout at them and shoo them outside, and sometimes I'd even hit one of them. Or I'd be sitting and writing and suddenly, instead of a cat meowing at the door to be let out, I'd hear the awful sound of innards being voided, and I'd see red and pick the cat up and smack it, or sometimes I'd drop it on the doorstep and send it arcing into the woods with a powerful kick. The other cats would immediately flee outside, where they'd cower in shame and guilt and I would stop writing and feel sorry for them. I couldn't write because I had struck a cat that I loved, I had kicked an innocent creature who meant everything to me, and sometimes, when in Prague, I'd feel such a sudden longing to see them that I'd drive out to Kersko and pick them up and press them to my forehead, so they could absolve me of my fears and my sorrow.

I was ashamed at what I'd done and I'd go outside and would sometimes spend the rest of the day trying to win back their trust, to get back into their good graces and persuade them to come back home. But those creatures were more deeply ashamed than I was and they were loath to go back to a place they'd been kicked out of, a place from which I'd driven them, because not only can cats feel deeply embarrassed, they cannot forgive as readily as I forgave them.

And it was strange, when I'd drive to the cottage by car, when I'd enter the Kersko forest and arrive at the spot where I turned into the lane leading to the cottage, I could see my cats come running in from the neighboring lots and gardens, so that by the time I pulled up to the gate, they'd all be standing there, beaming with delight that I'd come to be with them, that I'd made it, that I'd be giving them milk and food and taking them into my arms and finding consolation in each of them and giving each of them the courage to go on living, because these cats of mine may well have felt completely alive only when I was with them. And when I'd finished cuddling them and the weather was nice, I'd urge them to go outside and get some fresh air, to go and warm their coats, but I'd have to carry them out of the bedroom because they wouldn't have gone on their own. Their greatest delight was to be with me.

That week I didn't sleep over in Kersko because I didn't want to be there when the cats had their kittens. One day, I arrived to find the tabby cat missing, only to discover her in the woodshed where she'd given birth to five tiny kittens in a potato basket. She licked my hand and then, with her paws, she guided my fingers to her babies, who sucked at them, and they were as tiny as transistor radio batteries.

I stroked the kittens but was trembling with dread because the longer I allowed my hand to linger, the more I knew that this was the hand that would have to randomly choose some of those kittens and usher them out of this world. I felt the bile rise within me and my stomach began to ache. I poured out milk for the other cats and cut up pieces of meat for them, but when I sat down at the typewriter, I couldn't write, because my hands were shaking and I couldn't type a coherent sentence. I walked past the woodshed, followed by Blackie, who walked behind me because her belly, too, was enormous and she was close to her time. I squatted down and she hopped onto my knee and arched her back and nuzzled against me, seeking reassurance. I knew she was terrified of giving birth alone and wanted me to be with her when it happened.

I was disturbed because I could see the point-lessness of having come here. Kersko was not what my friends claimed it was, an ideal place to write and that I was lucky to have two places to live. In fact, the opposite was true. Whenever I was in Prague I worried about what my cats were doing and I couldn't write for fear they were hungry and alone. Then when I came to Kersko, I'd curse myself for not having stayed in Prague, because I couldn't write there, either. My wife, it seems, was beginning to make sense. What were we going to do with all those cats? I already had enough cats of my own and now I had an extra one who'd just given birth to five kittens, and Blackie would shortly be giving birth to five more.

An odd kind of inertia set in, making it impos-sible for me to be in Prague or Kersko, and since I was in Prague, I set out once more to Kersko to see the cats, and when I pulled up and got out of the car and the cats ran out to greet me, I knelt down and patted them but did not pick them up or press them to my face. I walked slowly under the birches, feeling aggravated and anxious because my favorite cat, Blackie, who was fondest of me and about whom I was crazy, had not come out to welcome me. I unlocked the door and poured out the milk and laid out the meat, and when I opened the window and looked out, I froze. There was Blackie lying in the bird feeder made from an old radio, and transmitting such an adoring look of love that I walked out of the house in a trance. When I reached the bird feeder, I saw that Blackie, too, had a litter of kittens, black and brindled, and she'd turned over on her back like a foundering battleship and was gazing at me lovingly, inviting me to behold the joy she'd brought to my parcel of land, that here, in the bird feeder, she was offering me her treasure, her five little kittens. I stuck my hand inside and Blackie licked it, and I rested my head on top of the feeder and held both hands out to Blackie, pressing my head on the old radio as though I were listening to news of fresh catastrophes in the world. I took a deep breath and tried to relax but couldn't quite manage it, so I remained there a while longer, my heart pounding, while the words my wife would utter to brighten my weekends in Kersko came into my head: 'What will we do with all those cats?'

I stepped back from the feeder and looked at Blackie, at her beautiful, adoring eyes bright with pride, then she turned on her side so the kittens could suckle more easily and I was so moved by her eyes and by the love flowing from those eyes to mine that I stuck my head into the feeder and Blackie and I touched noses and she licked me over and over again as if I were one of her kittens, and snuffled such sweet words of kitty love into my ears that I decided I would keep all of those kittens, come what may, and would offer five hundred crowns as a kind of kitty dowry to anyone who would agree to take one.

I brought Blackie some milk in a saucer, and she lifted herself up on her front legs and lapped it up, then I took the saucer to the woodshed for the tabby cat.

GUY DE MAUPASSANT

– *from* On Cats (1886) –

Translated from the French by Suzy Robinson (2021)

Guy de Maupassant (1850–1893) was a nineteenth-century French author. A protégé of Gustave Flaubert, he is best remembered as a master of the short-story form, and as a representative of the Naturalist school literary movement, which depicted human lives and destinies in disillusioned and often pessimistic terms.

Sitting on a bench the other day by my front door, in full sunlight, before a basket of flowering anemones, I was reading a recently published book; it was an honest book which is rare, and quite charming – *The Cooper* by Georges Duval. A large white cat belonging to the gardener leapt onto my lap, a sudden action which closed the book, which I then placed beside me so that I could stroke the beast.

It was hot; the scent of new flowers wafted through the air, a faint scent, intermittent and light, and occasionally there were cold gusts that came down from the vast white summits I could see in the distance.

But the sun burned down piercingly, one of those suns that penetrate the earth and give it life; a sun that cracks grain to awaken the sleeping sprouts, and makes buds open their young leaves. The cat rolled on my lap, on its back, its paws in the air, opening and closing its claws, displaying sharp fangs under its gums, and its green eyes in the almost-closed slits of its eyelids. I stroked and manhandled the soft, sinewy beast, supple as a silk cloth, soft, warm, delicious, and dangerous. She was purring delightedly and ready to bite, for she liked to claw as much as being flattered. She stretched out her neck, rippled, and when I stopped touching her, stood up and pushed her head under my raised hand.

I made her anxious and she also made me anxious, because I love them and I hate them, these charming and treacherous animals. I enjoy touching them, dragging under my hand their crackling and silky hair, feeling their warmth in this hair, this fine, exquisite fur. Nothing is softer, nothing gives the skin a more delicate, refined, rarer feeling than the warm and vibrant coat of a cat. But this living coat makes my fingers itch with a strange and ferocious desire to strangle the beast I caress. I feel the urge that she has to bite me and tear me, I feel it and I take it, this desire, like a fluid that she communicates to me; I take it through the ends of my fingers in this hot hair, and it goes up, it goes up along my nerves, along my limbs up to my heart, up to my head, it fills me, runs along my skin, makes my teeth clench. And always, always, at the tips of my ten fingers I feel the bright and light tickle that penetrates me and invades me.

And if the beast begins to bite me, and if it scratches me, I grab it by the neck, I spin it and throw it away like the stone of a slingshot, so fast and so brutally that it never has time to take revenge.

I remember that as a child, I already loved cats but with sudden urges to strangle them in my little hands; and that one day, at the end of the garden, at the entrance to the wood, I suddenly saw something grey rolling in the tall grass. I went to see; it was a cat caught at the collar, strangling, moaning, dying. He writhed, tore the earth with his claws, leaped, dropped inert and then began again, and his hoarse, rapid breath made a pumping sound, a terrible noise that I can to this day still hear.

I could have taken a spade and cut the collar, I could have gone to find a servant or told my father. No, I did not move, and with my heart beating, I watched him die with a quivering and cruel joy. It was a cat! If it had been a dog, I would have cut the copper wire with my teeth rather than let it suffer for a second more. And when the cat was dead, truly dead, still warm, I went to touch him and pull his tail.

Cats are delicious still, delicious above all, because in caressing them, while they rub our flesh, purr and roll over us, all the while looking at us with yellow eyes that never seem to see us, we feel the contingent nature of their tenderness, the treacherous selfishness of their pleasure.

JOHN KEATS

– To Mrs. Reynolds' Cat (1818) –

John Keats (1795–1821) is widely regarded as the most
talented of the second generation of English Romantic
poets. While his work was poorly received in his short
lifetime (he died of tuberculosis at the age of twenty-
five), today his poems and letters are among the most
popular – and most analysed – literary texts in the canon
of English literature.

C at! who hast pass'd thy grand climacteric,
    How many mice and rats hast in thy days
Destroy'd? – How many tit-bits stolen? Gaze
With those bright languid segments green, and prick
Those velvet ears – but pr'ythee do not stick
    Thy latent talons in me – and upraise
    Thy gentle mew – and tell me all thy frays
Of fish and mice, and rats and tender chick.
Nay, look not down, nor lick thy dainty wrists –
    For all thy wheezy asthma, and for all
Thy tail's tip is nick'd off – and though the fists
    Of many a maid have given thee many a maul,
Still is that fur as soft as when the lists
    In youth thou enter'dst on glass-bottled wall.

JAMES BOWEN

– *from* A Street Cat Named Bob
(2012) –

Born in 1979, English author James Bowen had a turbu-
lent childhood, and by spring 2007, he was enrolled on a
methadone programme, begging and busking in Covent
Garden and living in a supported housing programme.
One evening he returned home to find a ginger cat in the
hallway of his building. Assuming it belonged to another
resident, he simply returned to his flat, but when the cat
was still there the following day, and the day after that,
Bowen decided to help it.

I could feel Bob purring lightly as we walked
through the crowd towards Covent Garden.
He'd enjoyed the bus journey and now he was happily perched on my shoulder. I couldn't help smiling
to myself. I must look a bit like Long John Silver,
except I had a puss rather than a parrot sailing along
with me. Then, suddenly, I was aware of something.
Usually, no one would engage, or even exchange a
look, with me. I was a busker and this was London,
after all. But as I walked down Neal Street that afternoon almost every person we passed was looking at
me. Well, more to the point, they were looking at
Bob. It must have looked slightly strange, a tall, long-
haired bloke walking along with a large, ginger tom

on his shoulders. Not something you see every day – even on the streets of London.

Soon people started stopping us, asking to stroke Bob or take our photo. It made a nice change from being ignored, but it also meant that progress was pretty slow. By the time we got to Covent Garden it was almost an hour after I normally got set up. 'Can't afford to do this every day,' I grumbled to myself. By then, I'd been busking around Covent Garden for about a year and a half. I generally started at about two or three in the afternoon and carried on until around eight in the evening, to catch people on the way home from work. My main pitch was on a patch of pavement directly outside Covent Garden tube station on James Street. It could be a bit risky at times. Some people didn't like me approaching them and could be rude and even abusive at times. 'Piss off you scrounger'; 'Get yourself a proper job'. But that was always a part of being a busker. There were also plenty of people who were happy to hear me play a song, then slip me a quid. Busking at James Street was a bit of a gamble as well.

I was supposed to be on the eastern side of Covent Garden, near the Royal Opera House and Bow Street. James Street was meant to be the place for the human statues. But it was normally free, so I had made it my own little patch. I knew there was always the risk of getting moved along by the Covent Guardians. It was their job to police the Piazza and make sure the buskers and other entertainers had the right permits to perform – but I took my chances and it usually paid off. Huge numbers of people came out of the tube station. If only one in a thousand of them made a 'drop', then I could do OK. Arriving at the pitch, I first checked to make sure the coast was clear. There was no sign of the Covent Guardians. There were a couple of people who worked at the tube station who sometimes gave me hassle, because they knew I wasn't supposed to be there. But they didn't seem to be around either. So I put Bob down on the pavement near the wall and unzipped my guitar case.

Usually it would be a good ten minutes before people started to pay attention. Today though a couple of people slowed down in front of me and lobbed coins into my guitar case even before I'd played a note. Behind me I heard a male voice. 'Nice cat, mate.' I turned and saw a guy giving me a thumbs-up sign. I was taken aback. Bob had curled himself up in a comfortable ball in the middle of the empty guitar case and was already attracting a fair bit of silver. I knew he was a charmer, but this was something else. I'd taught myself to play the guitar when I was a teenager in Australia. I got my first guitar when I was fifteen or sixteen from a Cash Converters shop in Melbourne. I loved Jimi Hendrix and wanted to play just like him. The set I'd put together for my busking featured my heroes: Nirvana, Bob Dylan and a bit of Johnny Cash. The most popular song in my set was 'Wonderwall' by Oasis. That always worked best, especially outside the pubs when I wandered around later in the evenings. I'd barely been playing for more than a few minutes when a group of Brazilian kids stopped. One of them bent down and began stroking Bob. *'Ah, gato bonito,'* she said. 'She is saying you have a beautiful cat,' one of the boys translated. About half a dozen of the Brazilian kids and other passers-by began fishing around in their pockets and started dropping coins into the bag. I smiled at Bob. 'Looks like you may not be such a bad companion after all.'

As the late afternoon turned into the early evening and the crowds grew, more and more people were slowing down and looking at Bob. There was clearly something about him that attracted people. As darkness began to fall, a middle-aged lady stopped for a chat.

'You've found yourself a real friend there,' she said, stroking his fur.

'I think you're right,' I smiled.

She placed a fiver in the guitar case before leaving. I had been used to making around twenty pounds a session, which was enough to cover my expenses for a few days. But that night, it was clear that I'd made a lot more than that. When I finally totted it all up, I shook my head quietly. I had made the princely sum of £63.77. To most of the people that might not have seemed like a lot of money. But it was to me. I put all the coins in my rucksack and hauled it on to my shoulders. It was rattling like a giant piggy bank! I was ecstatic. That was the most I'd ever made in a day's work on the streets: three times what I'd make on a normal day. I picked up Bob, giving him a stroke on the back of the neck.

'Well done, mate,' I said. 'That was what I call a good evening's work.'

With the money we'd made I treated Bob to a nice pouch of posh cat food, a couple of packs of his favourite nibbles and some cat milk. I also treated myself to a curry and a couple of nice cans of lager.

'Let's push the boat out, Bob,' I said to him. 'It's been a day to remember.'

When we got home, Bob and I both wolfed down our food at lightning speed. I hadn't eaten so well in months – well, maybe years. I'm pretty sure he hadn't either.

– *from* A Story of Youth Told by Age (1939) –

Nikola Tesla (1856–1943) was a Serbian-American inventor, and electrical and mechanical engineer who was celebrated for his contributions to the design of the modern electricity supply system. He also claimed that his chastity was very helpful to his scientific abilities. In this arguably self-mythologising letter to a young woman, Miss Pola Fotitch, he tells of a seminal experience with his cat that first sparked his fascination with electricity.

Hotel New Yorker, 1939

My dear Miss Fotitch

I am forwarding to you the Calendar of Yugoslavia of 1939 showing the house and community in which I had many sad and joyful adventures, and in which also, by a bizarre coincidence, I was born.

As you see from the photograph on the sheet for June, the old-fashioned building is located at the foot of a wooded hill called Bogdanic. Adjoining it is a church and behind it, a little further up, a graveyard. Our nearest neighbours were two miles away. In the winter, when the snow was six or seven feet deep, our isolation was complete.

My mother was indefatigable. She worked regularly from four o'clock in the morning till eleven in the evening. From four to breakfast time – six am – while others slumbered, I never closed my eyes but watched my mother with intense pleasure as she attended quickly – sometimes running – to her many self-imposed duties. She directed the servants to take care of all our domestic animals, she milked the cows, she performed all sorts of labour unassisted, set the table, prepared breakfast for the whole household. Only when it was ready to be served did the rest of the family get up. After breakfast everybody followed my mother's inspiring example. All did their work diligently, liked it, and so achieved a measure of contentment.

But I was the happiest of all, the fountain of my enjoyment being our magnificent Macak – the finest of all cats in the world. I wish I could give you an adequate idea of the affection that existed between us. We lived for one another. Wherever I went, Macak followed, because of our mutual love and the desire to protect me. When such a necessity presented itself he would rise to twice his normal height, buckle his back, and with his tail as rigid as a metal bar and whiskers like steel wires, he would give vent to his rage with explosive puffs: *Pfftt! Pfftt!* It was a terrifying sight, and whoever had provoked him, human or animal, would beat a hasty retreat.

Every evening we would run from the house along the church wall and he would rush after me and grab me by the trousers. He tried hard to make me believe that he would bite, but the instant his needle-sharp incisors penetrated the clothing, the pressure ceased and their contact with my skin was gentle and tender as a butterfly alighting on a petal. He liked best to roll on the grass with me. While we were doing this, he bit and clawed and purred in rapturous pleasure. He fascinated me so completely that I too bit and clawed and purred. We could not stop but rolled and rolled in a delirium of delight. We indulged in this enchanting sport day by day, except in rainy weather.

In respect to water, Macak was very fastidious. He would jump six feet to avoid wetting his paws. On such days we went into the house and selected a nice cosy place to play. Macak was scrupulously clean, had no fleas or bugs, shed no hair, and showed no objectionable traits. He was touchingly delicate in signifying his wish to be let out at night and scratched the door gently for readmittance. Now I must tell you a strange and unforgettable experience that stayed with me all my life. Our home was about eighteen hundred feet above sea level, and as a rule we had dry weather in the winter. But sometimes a warm wind from the Adriatic would blow persistently for a long time, melting the snow, flooding the land, and causing great loss of property and life. We would witness the terrifying spectacle of a mighty, seething river carrying wreckage and tearing down everything moveable in its way. I often visualize the events of my youth, and when I think of this scene the sound of the waters fills my ears and I see, as vividly as then, the tumultuous flow and the mad dance of the wreckage. But my recollections of winter, with its dry cold and immaculate white snow, are always agreeable.

It happened that one day the cold was drier than ever before. People walking in the snow left a luminous trail behind them, and a snowball thrown against an obstacle gave a flare of light like a loaf of sugar cut with a knife. In the dusk of the evening, as I stroked Macak's back, I saw a miracle that made me speechless with amazement. Macak's back was a sheet of light and my hand produced a shower of sparks loud enough to be heard all over the house. My father was a very learned man; he had an answer for every question. But this phenomenon was new even to him. 'Well,' he finally remarked, 'this is nothing but electricity, the same thing you see through the trees in a storm.'

My mother seemed charmed. 'Stop playing with this cat,' she said. 'He might start a fire!' But I was thinking abstractedly. Is nature a gigantic cat? If so, who strokes its back? It can only be God, I concluded. Here I was, only three years old and already philosophising.

However stupefying the first observation, something still more wonderful was to come. It was getting darker, and soon the candles were lighted.

Macak took a few steps through the room. He shook his paws as though he were treading on wet ground. I looked at him attentively. Did I see something or was it an illusion? I strained my eyes and perceived distinctly that his body was surrounded by a halo like the aureola of a saint!

I cannot exaggerate the effect of this marvellous night on my childish imagination. Day after day I have asked myself 'what is electricity?' and found no answer. Eighty years have gone by since that time and I still ask the same question, unable to answer it. Some pseudo-scientist, of whom there are only too many, may tell you that he can, but do not believe him. If any of them know what it is, I would also know, and my chances are better than any of them, for my laboratory work and practical experience are more extensive, and my life covers three generations of scientific research.

– Cat and Mouse in Partnership (1812) –

Translated from the German by Margaret Raine Hunt (1886)

Jacob Ludwig Karl Grimm (1785–1863) and Wilhelm Carl Grimm (1786–1859) included this tale in the first edition of their *Kinder-und Hausmärchen*. This is one of the stories given to the brothers by Gretchen Wild (1787–1819), who lived with her sisters nearby.

A certain cat had made the acquaintance of a mouse, and had said so much to her about the great love and friendship she felt for her, that at length the mouse agreed that they should live and keep house together.

'But we must make a provision for winter, or else we shall suffer from hunger,' said the cat, 'and you, little mouse, cannot venture everywhere, or you will be caught in a trap some day.'

The good advice was followed, and a pot of fat was bought, but they did not know where to put it. At length, after much consideration, the cat said, 'I know no place where it will be better stored up than in the church, for no one dares take anything away from there. We will set it beneath the altar, and not touch it until we are really in need of it.'

So the pot was placed in safety, but it was not

long before the cat had a great yearning for it, and said to the mouse, 'I want to tell you something, little mouse; my cousin has brought a little son into the world, and has asked me to be godmother; he is white with brown spots, and I am to hold him over the font at the christening. Let me go out today, and you look after the house by yourself.'

'Yes, yes,' answered the mouse, 'by all means go, and if you get anything very good, think of me, I should like a drop of sweet red christening wine too.'

All this, however, was untrue; the cat had no cousin, and had not been asked to be godmother. She went straight to the church, stole to the pot of fat, began to lick at it, and licked the top of the fat off. Then she took a walk upon the roofs of the town, looked out for opportunities, and then stretched herself in the sun, and licked her lips whenever she thought of the pot of fat, and not until it was evening did she return home.

'Well, here you are again,' said the mouse, 'no doubt you have had a merry day.'

'All went off well,' answered the cat.

'What name did they give the child?'

'Top off!' said the cat quite coolly.

'Top off!' cried the mouse, 'that is a very odd and uncommon name, is it a usual one in your family?'

'What does it signify,' said the cat, 'it is no worse than Crumb-stealer, as your godchildren are called.'

Before long the cat was seized by another fit of longing. She said to the mouse,

'You must do me a favour, and once more manage the house for a day alone. I am again asked to be godmother, and, as the child has a white ring round its neck, I cannot refuse.'

The good mouse consented, but the cat crept behind the town walls to the church, and devoured half the pot of fat.

'Nothing ever seems so good as what one keeps to oneself,' said she, and was quite satisfied with her day's work. When she went home the mouse inquired,

'And what was this child christened?'

'Half-done,' answered the cat.

'Half-done! What are you saying? I never heard the name in my life, I'll wager anything it is not in the calendar!'

The cat's mouth soon began to water for some more licking.

'All good things go in threes,' said she, 'I am asked to stand godmother again. The child is quite black, only it has white paws, but with that exception, it has not a single white hair on its whole body; this only happens once every few years, you will let me go, won't you?'

'Top-off! Half-done!' answered the mouse, 'they are such odd names, they make me very thoughtful.'

'You sit at home,' said the cat, 'in your dark-grey fur coat and long tail, and are filled with fancies, that's because you do not go out in the daytime.'

During the cat's absence the mouse cleaned the house, and put it in order but the greedy cat entirely emptied the pot of fat.

'When everything is eaten up one has some peace,' said she to herself, and well filled and fat she did not return home till night. The mouse at once asked what name had been given to the third child.

'It will not please you more than the others,' said the cat. 'He is called All-gone.'

'All-gone,' cried the mouse, 'that is the most suspicious name of all! I have never seen it in print. All-gone; what can that mean?' and she shook her head, curled herself up, and lay down to sleep.

From this time forth no one invited the cat to be godmother, but when the winter had come and there was no longer anything to be found outside, the mouse thought of their provision, and said, 'Come cat, we will go to our pot of fat which we have stored up for ourselves – we shall enjoy that.'

'Yes,' answered the cat, 'you will enjoy it as much as you would enjoy sticking that dainty tongue of yours out of the window.'

They set out on their way, but when they arrived, the pot of fat certainly was still in its place, but it was empty.

'Alas!' said the mouse, 'now I see what has happened, now it comes to light! You, a true friend! You have devoured all when you were standing godmother. First top off, then half done, then –'

'Will you hold your tongue,' cried the cat, 'one word more and I will eat you too.'

'All gone' was already on the poor mouse's lips; scarcely had she spoken it before the cat sprang on her, seized her, and swallowed her down. Verily, that is the way of the world.

ALICE WALKER

– *from* Frida, The Perfect Familiar –

Born in 1944, Alice Walker is a Pulitzer-Prize winning
American novelist, short-story writer, poet and activist.
Best known from her novel *The Color Purple* (1982), for
which she won a National Book Award, she is also 'mature
enough' (as her daughter assures her) to own a cat.

S hortly after arriving in San Francisco I had been
fortunate, with the help of my partner, to find
a place in the country in which to dream, meditate,
and write. A year or so after being there I recon-
nected with the world of animals and spirits – in
trees, old abandoned orchards, undisturbed river-
banks – I had known and loved as a child. I became
aware that there is a very thin membrane, human-
adult-made, that separates us from this seemingly
vanished world, where plants and animals still speak
a language we humans understand, and I began to
write about the exhilarating experience of regaining
my childhood empathy. I discovered that not only is
there an adult-made membrane separating us from
animals, rocks, rivers and trees, ocean and sky, there
is one separating us from our remote ancestors, who
are actually so near that they are us. I began to write
The Temple of My Familiar, a book that immediately
became my home, just as the land I lived on became

the home of more and more animals, who, I sometimes joked with my partner, had somehow gotten
word that this was going to be a breakthrough book.
They seemed to know I had managed to poke a hole
through the membrane that separated me from
them, and they roamed the land: slithering, crawl-
ing, stalking, flying, in a steady, amazing wave. I've
written elsewhere of the captive horse looking for
refuge that suddenly appeared, the flocks of wild
turkeys, the feral pigs. The eagles, the snakes, and
the hawks. It really did seem as if word had gone
out: 'There's harmlessness over at Alice's!' I was in
heaven and I knew it; I realised that this experience
and others like it are 'the gold and diamonds and
rubies' of life on radiant earth.

On the day I finished the book, and while I still
lived in it as an ancestor who was very tight with a
lion, and as an even earlier ancestor who was a lion,
I saw a miniature 'lion' lying in the grass as I walked
up the hill to my studio. I knew it was time to invite
into my life another cat. My partner was sceptical,
reminding me of my poor track record. That I was
often on the road; that I can abide only a certain
amount of responsibility or noise. The yearning per-
sisted. I was only too aware of my limitations and
hesitated a year or more. I asked my daughter what
she thought: was I mature enough to have this antic-
ipated companion in my life? She thought yes.

And so the two of us began making the rounds

of shelters, looking at cats. Most had been abandoned, most were starved. Most were freaked-out but exhibited some degree of calm in whatever shelter they were in, where they were fed and kept dry and warm, and where, at the shelter we especially liked, there were young women and men who periodically opened the cages and brought the cats out for brushing, claw clipping, or a cuddle. It was here that we found Frida, a two-year-old long-haired calico with big yellow eyes and one orange leg. She was so bored with shelter life that on each of our visits she was sound asleep. Still, even in sleep, she had presence. We woke her up and took her home. Alas, like Willis, Frida was afraid of everything, even of caresses. She jumped at the slightest noise. For months she ran and hid whenever anyone, including me, came into the house. Brushing her was difficult because she could not abide being firmly held. Her long hair became shaggy and full of burrs. The guests who tried to pet her were scurried from; to show her dislike of them, she pooped on their bed. Much of her day was spent on the top shelf of a remote closet, sleeping.

I named her Frida, after Frida Kahlo. I could only hope she'd one day exhibit some of Kahlo's character. That despite her horrendous kittenhood she would, like Kahlo, develop into a being of courage, passion, and poise. When Frida wasn't sleeping, I discovered the Universe had played a very serious joke on me. Ever since I was a child I have needed the peace and quiet of morning. Everyone in my life, since I became an adult, has respected this. No one calls me, no one dares intrude for any reason, before noon. Frida made herself the exception. She was an exceedingly garrulous cat. She set out every morning to tell me the latest instalment of her sad, heart-rending tale, six or seven lives long, and she chatted steadily for an hour or so. When I was thoroughly rattled, she stopped, went upstairs, and took a nap. This was our entirely inauspicious beginning.

Being an activist means I travel, a lot. Sometimes to other cities and countries, but also between my city and country homes. I took to carrying Frida, when I could catch her, with me. I have memories of careening around mountain curves with Frida, terrified, stuck to my neck. I was unable to endure the piteous cries she emitted when I secured her in a cage. When not stuck to my neck or in my hair, she sought safety underneath the brake pedal. I eventually resolved to leave her in the country – she hid when she saw me packing to return to the city. I did this reluctantly, acknowledging defeat. I asked M, the caretaker, to make sure she had water, food, and surrogate affection. Time passed. Sometimes I would be away for a month or more. When I returned, Frida would have taken up at a neighbour's house. After a few days, she'd return. Distant and cool. I would struggle to renew our bond, beating myself up in my guilt. By the time we were back to the point of Frida's warily permitting a tentative stroke, I'd be off again.

Sometimes when I came home, she'd be hiding in the oak tree by the drive, or in the bay tree off the deck. If I brought anyone with me, she'd sit and watch us but never deign to appear. Sometimes when I returned, she'd simply cry. And cry and cry. It was a sound that went straight to my heart. And yet, this was my life. I thought perhaps Frida would one day simply get tired of it and leave me. She is very beautiful, very smart; I didn't think it impossible that she would, on her own, find a more suitable home. There were also times, after cleaning poop off the rug or the guest bed, that I wanted to help her relocate. More time passed.

One day I noticed that Frida understood English. If I said, 'I don't want you to lie on my chest because there's a book there at the moment that I'm reading,' and if I patted the spot by my thigh that was okay, she immediately settled there. If she knocked at the window and I said, 'Just a minute', she'd wait before coming to the door. I noticed that instead of dodging my caress, she sought it. On our walks, if I sat down to enjoy a view, she did too. Around that same time, I stopped criticising myself constantly for not being home all the time, or even most of it. If I was in too bad a mood to stroke or brush her and if, God forbid, I forgot to give her milk, which

I always brought and which she expected, I didn't think I was an awful person. I stopped worrying that somewhere there was probably a better companion than I was. We were the companion each of us had found, and I began to see that, in fact, we had a relationship.

Today Frida recognises the sound of my car, a sluggish black Saab convertible that chugs up the hill to our house, and on whose warm cloth top she likes to sleep. When I approach our gate, after the long drive from the city. I see her huge yellow eyes staring out beneath it. By the time I am out of the car she is at my side, chatting away. She accompanies me into the house, asking for milk, and as soon as I've put my things away, she stretches out on the rug in anticipation of a cuddle and a brush. If I'm not into her yet, she understands, and goes back to her milk or, with a querulous complaint, 'Where were you, anyhow? What took you so long?' she claims her favourite spot on the couch – which is everybody else's favourite too. When she sees me putting on boots and grabbing my walking stick, she leaps up, tail like a bushy flag, and beats me to the door. At first she talks as we walk, but then she falls silent, running alongside me exactly as a dog would. Sometimes she's distracted by field mice, but usually she does her hunting and gathering while I'm in the house; she likes to bring fresh mouse and leave it by the door. The little corpse, its neck chewed through, is, I know, Frida's bouquet. At night she watches me make a fire, plump the sofa pillows, lie down and cover myself with a quilt. She climbs promptly onto my chest and gives my breast a thorough kneading. This always makes me think of Frida's mother and wonder about her fate.

As the fire dances we listen to stories: Clarissa Pinkola Estés or Joseph Campbell; or music: Salif Keita, Youssou N'dour, Rachel Bagby. Bonnie Raitt, Tina Turner, or Al Green; Labi Siffre, Digable Planets, or Archie Roach; Phoebe Snow or Deep Forest; Sade. She likes music, except when it's loud. Purring, she stretches her considerable length – she is quite a big cat – and before falling asleep she always reaches up, with calm purpose, to touch my face. 'Watch those claws,' I always say. When it is bedtime I pick her up, cuddle her, whisper what a sweet creature she is, how beautiful and wonderful, how lucky I am to have her in my life, and that I will love her always. I take her to her room, with its cat door for her après-midnight exitings, and gently place her on her bed. In the morning when I wake up, she is already outside, quietly sitting on the railing, eyes closed, meditating.

– Cat-echisms –

There are two means of refuge from the misery of life – music and cats. – Albert Schweitzer

What greater gift than the love of a cat.
– Charles Dickens

If animals could speak, the dog would be a blundering outspoken fellow; but the cat would have the rare grace of never saying a word too much.
– Mark Twain

Time spent with a cat is never wasted. – Colette

It is good to be a cynic – it is better to be a contented cat – and it is best not to exist at all.
– H. P. Lovecraft

Authors like cats because they are such quiet, lovable, wise creatures, and cats like authors for the same reasons. – Robertson Davies

I believe cats to be spirits come to earth. A cat, I am sure, could walk on a cloud without coming through. – Jules Verne

No matter how much the cats fight, there always seem to be plenty of kittens. – Abraham Lincoln

I take care of my flowers and my cats. And enjoy food. And that's living. – Ursula Andress

Those who'll play with cats must expect to be scratched. – Miguel de Cervantes

I have studied many philosophers and many cats. The wisdom of cats is infinitely superior.
– Hippolyte Taine

A kitten is in the animal world what a rosebud is in the garden. – Robert Southey

If you really want to learn about life, get a cat.
– James Cromwell

I had been told that the training procedure with cats was difficult. It's not. Mine had me trained in two days. – Bill Dana

I have lived with several Zen masters – all of them cats. – Eckhart Tolle

Cats never strike a pose that isn't photogenic.
– Lilian Jackson Braun

The cat does not offer services. The cat offers itself.
– William S. Burroughs

A cat has absolute emotional honesty: human beings, for one reason or another, may hide their feelings, but a cat does not. – Ernest Hemingway

If you are worthy of its affection, a cat will be your friend, but never your slave. – Théophile Gautier

The smallest feline is a masterpiece.
– Leonardo Da Vinci

PERMISSIONS

Extract from *The Summer Book*, copyright © Tove Jansson, 1972, Moomin Characters™. Extract from *A Conversation with a Cat, and Others* by Hilaire Belloc reprinted by permission of Peters Fraser & Dunlop (www.petersfraserdunlop.com) on behalf of the Estate of Hilaire Belloc. *Pangur Bán* (The Monk and his Cat), translated by W. H. Auden, is reprinted by permission of the Estate of W. H. Auden. 'Letter to Hadley Mowrer, 25 November 1943' is taken from *Ernest Hemingway, Selected Letters 1917–1961*, edited by Carlos Baker. Copyright © 1981 by Carlos Baker and The Ernest Hemingway Foundation, Inc. Reprinted with the permission of Scribner, a division of Simon & Schuster, Inc. All rights reserved. Extract from *Making the Cat Laugh: One Woman's Journal of Single Life on the Margins*, copyright © 2010 by Lynne Truss, is reproduced by kind permission of Lynne Truss, HarperCollins UK and by kind permission of David Higham Associates. Extract from *Particularly Cats*, copyright © 1967 by Doris Lessing, is reproduced by kind permission of HarperCollins Publishers UK and HarperCollins Publishers. 'Mog the Cat and the Mysteries of Animal Subjectivity' by Naomi Fry, first published in *The New Yorker*, © Condé Nast, 2019. Extract from *Robinson*, copyright © 1958 by Muriel Spark, reproduced with kind permission of Birlinn Limited through PLSClear. Extract from *The Cat on My Shoulder: Writers and their Cats* reproduced by kind permission of Lisa Angowski Rogak, © Lisa Angowski Rogak, 1993. 'A Death in the Family' by Caitlin Moran reproduced by kind permission of *The Times* / News Licensing, copyright © 2017. Extract from *Jeoffrey: The Poet's Cat*, copyright © 2020 by Oliver Soden, reproduced by kind permission of the History Press.